PEN
ON A WIN

Kushal Choksi is an entrepreneur, a first-time author and a former Wall Street trader. After graduating from Carnegie Mellon University, he started his career at Goldman Sachs in New York City. Narrowly escaping death during the 9/11 attacks, he realized that life was too short to be playing safe. This got him started down the path of an eventful entrepreneurial journey, comprising of one failed venture and two successful acquisitions of an investment fund as well as a tech start-up. He currently runs Elements Truffles, an artisanal chocolate company that he co-founded with his wife. More about him at kushalchoksi.com.

ADVANCE PRAISE FOR THE BOOK

'An absorbing and enchanting breathwork bildungsroman that moves us from the meniality of modern corporate culture to the mesmerisms of meditation'—James Nestor, *New York Times* bestselling author of *Breath: The New Science of a Lost Art.*

'It's like *Autobiography of a Yogi* set in modern-day New York. It will stay in your heart long after you have put the book down'—Vishen Lakhiani, CEO, Mindvalley; author of *New York Times* bestseller *The Code of the Extraordinary Mind*, Nautilus Book Award winner.

'Like the WWII pilot forced to land his battle-damaged plane on "a wing and a prayer", Wall Street banker Kushal Choksi is forced by catastrophic events to embark on a remarkable journey of spiritual self-discovery. A poignant, funny, and thought-provoking read!'—Carol Kline, *New York Times* bestselling co-author of *Happy for No Reason, Love for No Reason*, five books in the *Chicken Soup for the Soul* series and *Conscious Luck: Eight Secrets to Intentionally Change Your Fortune.*

'Kushal delivers a powerful and earnest narrative of a curious mind's struggle to know what lies beyond the unknown and to find a purpose along the way'—Jeffrey Perlman, brand architect, former CMO, Zumba Fitness.

'Kushal's authentic journey of self-exploration inspires us all to question what it really means to lead a successful life. His heartfelt account will appeal to anyone seeking answers from within'—Chandrika Tandon, business leader, humanitarian and Grammy-nominated artist.

'*On a Wing and a Prayer* is a life-changing spiritual adventure. Deeply insightful and superbly written!'—Emma Seppälä, author of *The Happiness Track*; science director at Center for Compassion and Altruism Research and Education (CCARE), Stanford University.

ON A WING AND A PRAYER

SPIRITUALITY FOR THE RELUCTANT, THE CURIOUS AND THE SEEKER

KUSHAL M. CHOKSI

PENGUIN BOOKS

An imprint of Penguin Random House

PENGUIN BOOKS

USA | Canada | UK | Ireland | Australia
New Zealand | India | South Africa | China

Penguin Books is part of the Penguin Random House group of companies
whose addresses can be found at global.penguinrandomhouse.com

Published by Penguin Random House India Pvt. Ltd
4th Floor, Capital Tower 1, MG Road,
Gurugram 122 002, Haryana, India

Penguin
Random House
India

First published in Penguin Books by Penguin Random House India 2021

ISBN 9780143451679

Typeset in Adobe Garamond Pro by Manipal Technologies Limited, Manipal

www.penguin.co.in

For my father,
Madhukar P. Choksi,
my wings above the wind

Contents

I   *The Path before the Bend*

The Day Everything Changed   3

Floor 107. Cloud 9.   7

Get Out. Now.   11

Ring . . . Ring . . .   14

The Last One Out   17

The Aftermath   20

Life Owes You . . .   25

Cartesian Anxiety   29

Spiritual Shopping and Beyond   32

II   *When You're Ready, the Path Appears*

Sowing the Seed   39

Jack of All Meets Master of All   42

Contents

The Offer I Couldn't Refuse   51

Choiceless Unawareness   54

A Glimpse of SKY   57

Ready. Steady. Bang.   62

Mile Marker Seven   68

Wallflower in a Satsang   71

A Silent Scream   79

Renewing the Wow Factor   83

Four-Letter Word   87

III   *The Path Itself Is the Teacher*

Monk'i Mind   95

Red and Yellow Yoga Mats   99

False Sense of Control   106

I Didn't Listen   112

Leap. No Faith.   116

The Sign   119

The Ashram Life   123

Walk like a King   131

When It Rains   137

Laughing in Adversity   142

You Continue   148

Contents

On Faith   152

When He Asked and I Said . . .   158

Dancing on the Edge of a Sword   165

Real Virtual Reality   172

Eclipse and a Ball of Butter   181

The Chaos Theory   190

Power of Intention   194

He Is That   202

IV   *Strange Are the Ways of a Master*

The Wonder Years   209

Dealing with Boredom   214

He Was the Teacher Who Never Was   220

Love Me Do   226

Travelling Light   235

A Story of Success. A Story of Failure.   243

Soliloquy on Death   255

'Onipa'a   261

V   *Homecoming*

Wheel within a Wheel   269

Enlightenment Is For . . .   278

Contents

The Visitor Who Never Left   286

Visible Invisible Hand   292

Epilogue   299

Gratitude   303

Next Steps   307

I

The Path before the Bend

Pilot: 'Mayday. Mayday. Mayday.'

Control Tower: 'What's your local Bravo-17?'

Pilot: 'Seven miles south of the runway. A hole four feet square in the rudder, left engine spewing oil and flames. Nose shattered.'

'I'm coming in on a wing and a prayer . . .'

The Day Everything Changed

The Hudson was flowing gently, unaffected by the hustle on the island of Manhattan along the way. The commuter ferries criss-crossing the calm waters left ephemeral white lines in their wake. The sun once again rose behind the city skyline to outline its picturesque silhouette. Towards the southern end of this gorgeous profile stood two resolutely tall and perfectly symmetric sentries, as if guarding the frontier by the Atlantic Sea. I woke up to a New York City that appeared misleadingly cheerful on that late-summer morning.

The cogs of the gigantic capitalist machine had already started to pick up momentum by the time I left home. Armed with a copy of the *Financial Times* in one hand and an oversized cup of coffee in the other, I ran through a mental checklist of the conversations I had to have and targets I needed to meet. In that regard, I was probably no different from the milieu of people on their way to work in the dream city.

Every day, a short commuter train ride would bring me to the transportation hub in the bowels of the World Trade Center. A long escalator ride up to the mezzanine floor and a brisk walk alongside the shops on the ground level. Cutting across the Tobin Plaza while greeting the majestic cast-bronze mural. And from there, a short westward trek down Fulton Street towards Old Slip to the office building overlooking the East River.

That morning, I would ominously deviate from my religiously travelled routine.

I loved what I did. At a very young age, Wall Street had sprung open the doors to the famed 'American dream' that I was determined to achieve as a hyper-ambitious Indian immigrant. I was so focused on getting there, that at some point along the way I stopped asking exactly what I was chasing, why I wanted it, or whether I really wanted it at all. At that time, it felt strangely right.

I ascended the escalator and began my predictable journey. My body was navigating the mezzanine floor of the World Trade Center, but my mind was in its own virtual reality—flooded with thoughts about my never-ending work, my demanding boss, an argument with my girlfriend . . .

BAANNNNNGGGGG! A deafening sound pulled me out of my reverie.

It was a massively high-decibel blast, followed by a ghastly hissing sound. It was as if a high-pressure steam pipe had just burst open. All I recall about that chilling moment is that it was dreadfully frightening. Not knowing how to react, people around me were screaming in fright, and a frenzied dash for the exit doors had commenced. A moment ago, the world was spinning as usual, but in the blink of an eye, it had completely changed—just like the unsuspecting, colourless liquid in a chemical experiment instantaneously turns pink with one more drop of a titrant. And in that moment, I was suddenly and forcefully ejected out of my own virtual reality. At one level, besides the frightful sound, there were no signs of anything out of place. Yet, the swarm of commuters was gripped by the fear of the unknown.

'A bomb has gone off. It's mayhem here.' I overheard a gentleman screaming down the phone while he ran for the door. At a distance, a lady tripped while running, and that caused a stampede. Men who would otherwise hold the door for that lady were now stepping over her just to get to the exit first. A strange fear of an imminent end had gripped the atmosphere. At that moment, my entire life flashed before me. A fleeting thought crossed my mind— *perhaps this is it for me.*

As I somehow made my way to the exit, I was stopped by a security guard cajoling the river of people gushing outside to stay within the building.

'Everyone, stay inside. It is unsafe outside these doors. Go back inside and be safe.' The concern in his blaring voice was clear. I stopped in my tracks, debating whether to heed his instructions. Just then, someone tapped my shoulder from behind.

Floor 107. Cloud 9.

'Welcome to Goldman Sachs. You are one of the chosen few. You have been through the rigour and I'm sure you now have an appreciation of what it takes to be here.' Some big head of quant trading began his rousing welcome speech to a room full of hungry hopefuls. He had an air of geeky confidence around him. A dark, bespoke suite hugged his sculpted body. His left eye twitched as he spoke. Besides his Maths PhD laurels, what qualified him to speak to us was perhaps the fact that he made seven-figure bonuses in his mid-thirties. He was sent to rile up gladiator spirits. And boy, was he doing a fine job. I had arrived with my aspirations to a place where aspirations barely stood out.

We were the analyst batch of 2000 from New York, London and Tokyo. Little did we know that very soon, the camaraderie in the room would give way to cut-throat rivalry. All of us would soon be pitched against each other in the prestigious trading competition.

'You all come from reputed schools where the competition is dog-eat-dog. It's the other way around in our industry.' A few in the room chuckled, though not everyone got his sarcasm. Angus, my buddy from the UK office who was sitting next to me whispered naively, 'Mate . . . the other way around is still dog-eat-dog . . .' I ignored him. My entire being was busy absorbing every word coming out of the big mouth of the big boss.

After the three-month training, I would soon join the quant desk. This group of quants—short for quantitative analysts—were tasked with coding mathematically complex algorithms that crunched a lot of numbers and distilled unimaginable amounts of information into simple decisions of buying low and selling high. Until that point, I had not formally studied financial mathematics. But I wasn't complaining.

Every morning, I would look forward to getting to work early and revving up the engines of these models that would then cause millions of dollars to slosh around throughout the day. As a structural engineer trained to design load-bearing arches for bridges and tunnels, I would often question, but mostly be amused by, how easily the world of financial trading was able to create perceived value out of thin air just by pushing some buttons on a keyboard. Moreover, the entirely self-fulfilling hypothesis made it all look very important.

Regardless of the inherent vanity, it was somewhat difficult to ignore the ego-boosting perception that if you wore fancy suits and Ferragamo ties to work, you must be doing something important. It was a stunning and well-choreographed circus.

'Working here, you all have a premium on you. And you can cash it but once.' The arrogance in his statutory warning was difficult to miss. He was motivating, educating and intimidating all of us newbies in the same breath.

It was serendipitous enough how I ended up on Wall Street. I hadn't even heard of the famed investment bank when they came to interview on campus. However, the invisible hand of destiny pushed me to a part of Carnegie Mellon University's leafy campus that day where I happened to run into a classmate who had just walked out battered and bruised from the interview. 'These people are crazy. And ruthless,' he said. It sent a curious tickle down my spine. I dashed to the interview office only to find that all the interview slots were full. I begged for an opportunity. The kind lady behind the desk apologized and encouraged me to try next time. But there was no next time! We were all graduating soon. Later that evening, I got a call. Apparently, someone had dropped out and one slot had opened up.

'So then get ready. See you all at 7 a.m. tomorrow at Windows on the World,' the big boss bellowed.

'Floor 107 of the World Trade Center. Best dirty martinis at the bar next door, mate.' Angus whispered in giddy excitement. He somehow knew that I had no clue where this place was. Over the next three months, we would all spend a lot of time in that large meeting hall, bonding intimately with the towering space overlooking the majestic island of Manhattan and beyond. From there, one could see airplanes at eye level as they glided on their final approach into LaGuardia airport. What if one ever made a wrong left turn? I never wondered.

I was the runner up on the board for the trading competition. Unfortunately, there was no recognition for second place.

Get Out. Now.

Amidst rising chaos and against the backdrop of loud security instructions, I turned around to see whose hand had found my shoulder.

His face was vaguely familiar.

'Don't listen to the guard. Let's just get the hell out of the building and run.' He said with the conviction of a Marine Corps infantry leader.

Despite all that was going on, I managed to show my annoyance at this fellow who was telling me to walk out when a lot of people were listening to instructions and turning around.

'I don't care what this guard says. Just listen to me. Let's get out of here. It's the right thing to do.' He reiterated forcefully.

His voice was too loud to ignore, and it carried a strange force. I don't know what it was, but my feet obeyed without much resistance. I took a deep breath and followed his lead to step out.

It was raining. An unruly mix of glass splinters, cement chips, shreds of insulation and paper scraps were coming down in a grey haze. Deafening sirens filled the atmosphere. City firefighters, known for their near-perfect swiftness, courage and agility, had taken command and started making their way into the building in a single-file line. I managed to walk a couple of blocks and found safe harbour under the awning of a deli. By now, I had heard people talking about a plane having crashed into the building.

As someone who grew up tapping into the radio frequencies of air traffic controllers with my ham radio and listening to their conversations with pilots, I immediately began to imagine all that could have gone wrong inside a cockpit for an aircraft to be involved in a collision at such a low altitude on a clear day. It didn't add up. In that moment of incoherence, I could now clearly see a few people hanging out of the windows, trapped by the smoke and flames gushing out of the North Tower.

As my senses tried to decipher what was going on, my companion seemed to have vanished.

In that moment, nothing made sense. How does a plane crash into a building like that? What should I do next? Should I inform my colleagues that I would be late for the meeting? How do I reach my family? Ironically, I had left my cell phone at work the day before. My brain was in overdrive. Somehow, I managed to borrow a phone from a stranger. I had to call Alak.

Ring . . . Ring . . .

The first time our paths crossed was on the very first day of my undergrad. That is also when I instinctively knew that I would somehow end up with her. Later on, I figured that perhaps my instincts had been wrong, as our circumstances and preferences turned out to be starkly different—let's just say we were two very different individuals with little in common.

Our eyes met for the first time on a dusty road by the main admin building of the university campus. We smiled as if we had known each other for a long time. But then we resumed walking in our own separate directions. I turned around to look at the comet that had just blazed past me. She kept walking. Soon I found out that she was already with someone, but I was never the type to give up. I remained hopeful. As hope began to fade with time, I unsuccessfully tried finding a meaningful relationship. And just like that, for the next several years, we kept walking further away from each other.

Fate again brought us closer after we both migrated to the US. We began talking. It started with letters. Then texting back and forth from the Unix prompt of a vintage PC in the university's computer lab. Then talking on the phone when I could afford one. And eventually, meeting in person. She spoke and I listened. Conversations with her fascinated me then just like they do now. There was grace and innocence in her every move. There was simplicity and confidence. Humility and razor-sharp intelligence. She later went on to become a trader at Goldman Sachs. Our area of work overlapped quite a bit—but we never ever talked about work.

While we were very different individuals, we shared basic values. Like a dovetail joint, there was a symmetry in us. We cared deeply for one another and looked after each other's blind spots.

We talked about simple things. We talked about life. We wondered how we had come together against all odds from our seemingly divergent paths. We would run Monte Carlo simulations on a future that was not so deterministic. We dreamt of leaving the rat race some day and starting a little chocolate shop somewhere in a charming old town in Europe. We talked about beauty in simple things.

She was jealous of my books, for I could disconnect fully and vanish into my own world with them. She wouldn't let me read. She'd rather that I talked to her. It would annoy me, but resistance was futile. Our conversations were the bedrock of our relationship.

That day I wanted to talk, but she wouldn't pick up the phone. In that state of exasperation and disbelief, I didn't know whether to laugh or cry. I left her a frantic message. In the heat of the moment, I even reprimanded her for missing out on what could have been our last opportunity to talk. I regretted saying that later.

'Enough. I need to run.' The hurried and harried stranger snatched the phone I had borrowed. Very soon, the entire telephone network would collapse, erasing any possibility of communication whatsoever, leading my loved ones to imagine the absolute worst.

The Last One Out

I would later find out that American Airlines Flight 11 had crashed into the North Tower, killing everyone on board and hundreds of others in the building. The fire had started to build now. Plumes of black smoke gushed out of the building.

Just then, I saw birds taking flight and nose diving towards me. A few of us noticed and instinctively started moving backwards, without taking our eyes off them. However, in no time, it became clear that we were not on their trajectory. A few seconds later, to my horror, I realized that they were not birds, but people jumping out of the top floors. They had to make a choice between being asphyxiated inside or ending their lives wilfully. The anguish and pain of that moment was lodged like a splinter of glass in my consciousness.

I stood there thunderstruck, caught in a whirlwind of the perfect storm.

And then, before I could stabilize myself, another aircraft appeared out of nowhere and penetrated the southern façade of the South Tower with an ear-splitting sound. The impact, and the instantaneous combustion of fuel, spit out a massive ball of fire on the other side of the building. My stumped brain was now on the verge of giving up. A gentleman in front of me fainted and began to stumble in my direction. I caught his arm and eased him to the ground. Pandemonium had peaked inside and outside.

Before I could be consumed by fatalistic thoughts of an apocalypse, I remembered the instructions to run as far away as possible from this bedlam. I began a determined dash towards the east side of the island.

Just as I reached Water Street on the other side of Manhattan, a ghastly rumble was heard in the distance. The rumble turned into an ear-piercing roar, growing more intense every second. An enormous cloud of debris and smog was moving rapidly towards me, engulfing everything and everyone along the way. The North Tower of the World Trade Center was collapsing.

At a distance, a commuter ferry was pulling out of Pier 11. I ran towards it with all my might. The gangway had already been pulled in. The captain saw me running towards the boat. He paused. My momentum allowed me to leap on board.

The ferry pulled back. The cloud of dust and debris came so close to me and, almost as if disappointed that it missed me, it swirled around and enveloped the entire skyline in its angry grasp. As I stared blankly at the frothy waters that the vessel left behind, it occurred to me that I was the last person on the last boat leaving Manhattan that day.

The boat set-off towards Weehawken, New Jersey. As the vessel turned around the tip of the island, there was a collective gasp of disbelief from the people on board. The North Tower had been razed to the ground and the South Tower was ablaze. An agonizing silence consumed everyone around me. Moments later, the silence was violated by the hair-raising crash of the South Tower. Like a fragile house of cards, the second tower came down right in front of our eyes. This had turned into an endless nightmare that I could not wake up from.

The sequence of events and the speed at which everything happened was mind-numbing. What if I had simply listened to that well-meaning security guard who had pleaded with everyone to stay inside the building, citing safety? I have no idea whether he made it out alive that day. I hope he did. What if I too had perished in that virulent grey haze? What would have happened to my family? My career? All those dreams and aspirations? Suddenly, everything that my life had been based on just a few hours ago appeared trivial and unreal.

A state of nothingness ensued over the next few days. I had become a statistic. A 9/11 survivor.

The Aftermath

The entire city of Weehawken appeared confused. All modes of transportation had come to a standstill, just as all the thoughts in one's head occasionally cease to exist. Phone networks were non-functional. Everyone, without exception, was walking around with a blank look of disbelief. A kind lady handed me a tissue. I wasn't sure why. Then I realized my nose was bleeding.

The motives of the attack were now somewhat clear, but in no way did this help reality to sink in. I walked for nearly four hours through the doom and gloom to get home.

On my way home, I managed to call Alak from a public pay phone. 'I'm safe.' That's all I told her. 'Let me get home first.' I was having trouble completing my sentences.

She had stayed in touch with my family. I still wasn't able to speak to them. I tried to reach them a few times but got the familiar pre-recorded message stating that all the lines were busy.

My roommate Tola screamed when he saw me, as if he'd seen a ghost. Mixed emotions of relief and disbelief were palpable in his expression. He had been trying to reach me for quite some time and by now had played and replayed every possible scenario in his head. He hugged me tight. I think that was the first time he had embraced me. He went on and on about how he saw the planes hit from his office in Jersey City across the river. I could see his lips move but his words didn't travel past my ear canal. Nothing was registering. Absolutely nothing was making sense.

I tried to sleep but I couldn't. An everyday sound like the hard closing of a door was enough to jolt me off-centre. I was wired. And tired. And hungry. But I couldn't make myself get out of bed. I just lay there listlessly for some time, until the loud ringing of the landline stirred me out of my dazed state. It was my family friends from Mumbai. They too were relieved to hear my voice. I couldn't hold a simple conversation until the end. I hung up.

I have no recollection of meeting my parents for the first time. And an equally low understanding of the precise nature of the application process in the heavens to choose parents. That said, being born to my mother and father was—in the words of Warren Buffet—like winning an 'ovarian lottery'. I was a late child, as my mother had waged war with nature to bring me into this world.

And despite all the odds that nature had stacked against her, she had prevailed. She didn't have to struggle as hard for my kid sister, and so in bouts of intense verbal sparring as children, I often accused my sister of having arrived uninvited.

Despite our many casual disagreements, one thing we both cherish, even today, is our childhood. A happy upbringing in a cocoon of love.

I grew up in a religious family. My grandmother would spend most of her day in prayer and meditation. She would often ask me to read her a page or two from ancient Vedic scriptures. My mother followed her lead. My mother's faith and devotion to her path were impeccable. As children, we were never forced to follow any rituals, and that freedom alone, I believe, was enough to sow the seed of acceptance towards spirituality.

Amongst many other things, my father passed on a deep love for books. The only difference between us was that he actually finished every book he picked up. His journey from the tiny, non-descript village of Dhandhuka in India to graduate school at Stanford University was a matter of wonder as well as inspiration for me. Fortune forced him to abandon his comfortable life in the US and immigrate back to India to take care of his family. I can't imagine that to be a happy outcome, but I never heard him grumble about it. I wish I had somehow inherited that unconditional acceptance. But today, the situation was different. My mother had nearly fainted when she couldn't reach me for some time, and so my father too was dealing with his own 9/11, some 8,000 miles away in India.

I decided to get away from this godforsaken place to see Alak, who happened to live in Raleigh, North Carolina then. Every aircraft in the country was grounded. Desperate and out of options, I took to the road, buying a one-way ticket on a Greyhound bus. I had never been on one before. I had only experienced them in Simon and Garfunkel songs.

I boarded around midnight. The rear of the bus was humid and smelled of deep-fried chicken. I was perhaps the only brown-skinned fellow on the bus that night. Time and again, I felt violated with the piercing looks of disdain and disapproval from fellow passengers during what turned out to be the longest silent road trip of my life. For the first time in my life, I felt discriminated against in the country I had come to love and cherish so much—especially for what it stood for. I wanted to scream at the top of my lungs, 'I may have the same skin colour as those guys but besides that I have nothing to do with this. I have more in common with you all than with them!' But of course, I kept quiet.

My vibrating phone woke me up an hour or so before the bus reached its destination. The rays of the rising sun were attempting to make their way in through the dirty windowpane to my left. It was my boss. After inquiring about my wellbeing, he didn't waste much time in asking me when I could report back to work. In less than twenty-four hours, Goldman Sachs had already set up a command centre and make-shift trading floor at One New York Plaza. After all, the expected jump in volatility would present numerous opportunities for money to be made once the markets opened in a couple of days. Bravo.

I couldn't comprehend such a rapid shift in the collective consciousness. This was not the US I had dreamed of or had ever experienced before. Like a delicate free-spirited child feeling hardened and insensitive after experiencing horrific abuse, the atmosphere of the country had changed in the blink of an eye. And there I stood, mute and dazed in the eye of the storm, watching my world heading in the direction of the slow-moving, frequently stopping bus that night. South.

Life Owes You . . .

It had been exactly one week. Normalcy was trying to force its way back in. My commute had changed. The station I would usually disembark at was now covered in ashes and rubble. The burning smell still engulfed the air. That day on the ferry, speeding towards lower Manhattan, I sat with my eyes closed. The chilly water of the Hudson was splashing indiscriminately on the hull of the boat. On a normal day, my mind would be planning ahead and running through an infinitely long checklist. But that day, I wasn't interested. Like trying to lift a paralyzed limb, I just couldn't force myself to be normal. I couldn't care less. My mind was wandering aimlessly. My body was still. And yet, I was already exhausted.

Was this *Smashana Vairagya*? A Sanskrit term, which loosely translates to the surreal dispassion that sets in when one encounters death at close quarters. A state in which one questions everything and wonders about the sheer meaninglessness of it all. Whatever it was, I could neither bear it, nor get completely rid of it.

As my enthusiasm for life was slowly fading away, my thoughts continued to oscillate back and forth in a desperate search for resonance. Then one night, while tossing and turning in bed, it suddenly hit me. Up until this point, I had been living inside a warm and comfortable cocoon, which had now been ripped to shreds. Whatever I was chasing or holding on to until this point suddenly held little significance in my mind. Everything I had thought about myself and the expectations I had from life had turned to ashes. What was the purpose of all that I had strived so hard for? The dream home, the perfect car, the ideal soulmate . . . all that could have vanished like smoke in thin air, leaving no trace. Was this world a massive charade, or an illusion? Did I want to ultimately forget that this ever happened, and return to doing more of the same? Suddenly, all my aspirations and well-laid future plans appeared inconsequential, shallow and meaningless.

In a way, nothing had really changed. I was still in the same job, same relationship, had the same bank account, drove the same car, had the same healthy body. Yet at some level, my world had changed in the most unanticipated way.

When everything is going hunky-dory and suddenly life hits you with a club in the head, the shooting pain brings up some deep questions. What is the real purpose of life? Am I really doing what I'm meant to do? And the answer is almost always inconclusive.

Suddenly life appeared too short to ignore my inner voice—it seemed quite a waste to not follow what the heart really wanted. But what did my heart really want?

However romantic that notion of following my inner voice appeared to be, where rubber met the road, it felt very scary. I wanted to listen to my inner voice, but what was that voice saying? It was too muffled, there was so much static in there. I could barely make out what it was asking me to do. Life was staring at me without winking, like a mean beast who had not yet decided what to do with me.

And then the journey began. Based on what I had seen others do, my conditioned mind desperately wanted to quit the rat race, give up the nine-to-five drudgery, travel the world, be like the monk who sold his Ferrari, do something that would create a dent in the universe, and all that jazz. There was a barrage of thoughts, and each thought was more compelling than the previous one. Each had its own pros and cons.

This was the first time in my life I felt so suffocated inside. I was no longer in control of my thoughts, my emotions, or of anything for that matter. I should have been happier to be alive and kicking. However, the feeling that everything I had been chasing so far was utterly meaningless created the sensation of fighting a losing battle in a claustrophobic boxing ring. It reminded me of my first swimming lesson, when the heartless coach had thrown me into the deep end of the pool, and I was left gulping down copious amounts of chlorinated water.

I felt complete at some level, and yet I had tremendous inner turmoil. There was mild enthusiasm for the journey ahead, but behind that lurked a hesitation to start anything new, for fear that the curtains would be drawn in the middle of the act.

My mind kept replaying the sequence of events, much like a radio tune you pick up on your way to work. Only this time, it wasn't pleasant. A putrid burning stench and a veil of smoke enveloped downtown Manhattan for months, just as my mind remained foggy and pessimistic. Nightmares became frequent.

At one level, I was grateful for the new lease of life, yet at another level, it felt like having the wrong currency in a foreign country. I didn't know what to do with it.

And that's when I realized that life didn't owe me anything.

Cartesian Anxiety

Time has a healing quality, and a routine is an anaesthetic. Together, both can restore an apparent sense of normalcy rather quickly—at least, on the surface. A resilient city like New York only makes the process easier. The impact of the event began to fade away, albeit at a glacial pace. Just like a frozen lake, however, what lay beneath was not the same as the icy, meditative surface.

When faced with such a predicament, the human mind generally seeks a distraction, so that it does not have to deal with the discomfort inside. A concoction of conflicting sentiments continued to brew within me. My mind was confused, and I was gripped by the disturbing feeling that life was too short, and that I must try everything there was before it was too late. An artificial sense of urgency was born.

I had studied René Descartes, a celebrated philosopher and mathematician, and now I was living his work.

Cartesian anxiety is the notion that the study of the world as something separate from ourselves can lead to a firm and unchanging knowledge about ourselves. Much like an inward exploration.

I took to traveling and exploring the world with Alak. I would look for the most off-the-beaten-track places on the planet, and whenever we had the time, we would simply pack our bags and go. The more difficult or out of the way a place was, the more gratifying it seemed and the longer the distraction lasted in my mind. The heart loves simple things, but the mind seeks challenges.

We spent time exploring the Amazonian rainforests and cacao farms of Ecuador. We walked the footsteps of the legendary Don Quixote in Castilla La Mancha of Spain, reliving the fame and misfortune of the famed hidalgo I had fallen in love with as a child. We spent weeks backpacking the difficult and virgin terrains of Torres Del Paine near the southern tip of the world, tracing Magellan's journey. We explored history in Europe, culinary interests in Asia, and Mayan culture and the art of indigenous Americans in Central America. We walked the glaciers, dove the blue oceans of the Caribbean in search of coral reefs, and saw the most magnificent sunrises after scaling mountain tops.

Nothing worked. The restlessness continued to spread like a pandemic within.

I started driving fast cars and running marathon distances. Still unfulfilled, I began experimenting with cooking and music. I picked up my guitar, which had gathered considerable dust since college. Ironically, I even began learning to fly an airplane. Despite all of this, I was losing interest and enthusiasm.

I wasn't depressed. I was just bored and disinterested. And I was fully aware of it.

Spiritual Shopping and Beyond

The conflict inside me was becoming more and more pronounced—and harder to ignore. On the one hand, I had this apathy for life, and on the other, a yearning to pursue unfinished business and passions, all at great speed. Life was fleeting.

I began to realize that in my search for solace, external distractions did not bring me any closer to contentment. This was a clear reminder that action doesn't necessarily equate with progress.

My father, a voracious reader, had read and collected a lot of literature published by Osho, also known as Acharya Rajneesh—a new-age Indian spiritual teacher with a considerable following in India and in the US back in the eighties. Dad would bring home VHS tapes from an Osho centre near my home during my high school days. He would watch his talks. I couldn't fully understand what Osho was saying because my English wasn't strong enough to grasp everything. Moreover, at fourteen, I did not appreciate the spiritual exactitude in his spellbinding style. But his oration was riveting. I would put my school books down and just keep listening to him, regardless of whether I understood it fully or not. Years later, I hitchhiked my way to his ashram in Pune, India.

During this current period of internal conflict, I recalled that part of my life and turned to Osho again. His talks and books were intellectually stimulating and thought-provoking. This time, I made more ground on taking it all in.

At that time, his emphasis on living in the moment was new to me. Practicing awareness and not letting my mind slip between the future and the past sounded extremely logical, timely and therapeutic. But how? How was I supposed to tell my mind to live in the moment? It was anyway witnessing a tremendous battle between two polar-opposite points of view. How was I to instruct my mind? The more I instructed my mind, the more it decided to rebel.

Whenever I would close my eyes to meditate, either thousands of unsettling thoughts would gush in, and I'd get exhausted trying to stop them, or I would just fall asleep.

A friend of mine suggested that I listen to Osho's Mahageeta—his commentary on a highly-evolved conversation between an enlightened sage named

Ashtavakra and a mighty king named Janaka. With great enthusiasm, I brought home the more than thirty volumes of the commentary. I couldn't listen past the first two.

Besides the intellectual rigour, I found the entire exercise to be dry. The knowledge remained a foreign and ethereal concept, which did not become my living experience. Essentially, I could not internalize it all. Eventually, I couldn't bear the weight of my spiritual unease, and so I dropped it. Perhaps I wasn't ready.

I began reading about Swami Vivekananda, a saint born in India. His practical wisdom and his relationship with his master struck a chord inside me. I started frequently visiting the Vedanta Society of New York on the Upper West Side. While his teachings created a deeper curiosity, for some reason, I soon lost interest there as well.

Meanwhile, on the professional front, I was rising fast. I was now a vice president at Goldman Sachs' prestigious asset management group. According to the veterans at the firm, this was the shortest time anyone had ever taken to get this far from the lowest rung of the ladder. The head of the asset management business called me into his office. He congratulated me on the promotion and assured me that I had a star-studded road ahead if I kept going at this pace.

'I see what you have done for yourself in a short period of time. Just hang in there. It will be worth it'—the parting words of the big boss ring clearly in my head even today.

I quit three months later.

Life is too short to not be doing things that one really wants to do. The very seed of this clichéd thought had become a little sapling by now. I had silently quit a promising career in search of a path less travelled. A path that promised more thrill.

I joined a nondescript—yet promising—investment firm, which had neither any capital nor any track record. My friends and colleagues snubbed it as a quixotic and foolish move, but I couldn't be swayed. It just felt right at that point. I was determined to follow my heart and to not feel compelled to take the safer route.

And just like that, life kept waltzing between feelings of wanting to experience everything and swiftly getting bored of everything. Like a snowflake fractal—fragile and evidently symmetric on the surface, but full of chaos and infinite randomness within—my life was simply flowing with time.

I was now married to Alak. For one who refused to look her age and the other who refused to behave his age, we were happy and living life as an adventure, one day at a time. From an onlooker's perspective, life was perfect. But there was a hole in my soul.

And then the unexpected happened.

II

When You're Ready, the Path Appears

What you seek is seeking you.

—Rumi

Sowing the Seed

Walking through New York City is a rousing experience. One is exposed to so many different aspects of life while ambling through the streets of this extreme city. On the same block, you see an immaculately dressed woman with a groomed dog and a homeless man with a cardboard sign that begs for attention—both immersed in their own realities. On the same street, a fine limo and an impatiently honking yellow cab. On the same corner, an overbearing smell of incense from the table of a street hawker who sells fake Prada and the nauseating smell of garbage. A fine dining restaurant with a prix fixe menu and a bodega next door, where one could buy a week's worth of groceries for the same price. A brilliant art installation on the least expected corner and graffiti-laden walls as you turn that very corner. A finely appointed historic brownstone building and a modern luxury high-rise. And a silent witness to all, a zebra crossing that is periodically flooded with a river of pedestrians once the small backlit sign on a pole turns to WALK.

Alone in this crowd, one could often spot two friendly faces—Alak and Shubhra. Colleagues and friends at Goldman Sachs, they waded through this organized chaos twice a day as part of their commute. Like two schoolchildren, oblivious of their overly stimulating surroundings. They would talk about everything under the sun—from mean bosses to the meaning of life. It was the part of her daily routine that Alak would look forward to.

Once, during their evening walk back home, Shubhra invited us to a meditation event with her spiritual teacher, Gurudev Sri Sri Ravi Shankar, who was visiting New York City from India in a couple of weeks. Alak brought it up at dinner that night, and my knee-jerk reaction was to pour a glass of cold water on the proposal.

I had heard a little bit about Sri Sri, but I wasn't really interested in going. I was averse to gurus.

Besides, that Saturday I had planned to work. Back then, I was developing a financial model that wasn't behaving as expected, and I was pretty sure that the behemoth would consume all of my precious weekend.

However, buried somewhere under the layers of resistance was a seed of curiosity. Later that night, I googled him. People largely referred to him as Sri Sri or Gurudev. There was quite a bit of scattered information out there. His picture looked strangely familiar, and he had a warm, gentle smile. He was the founder of the Art of Living Foundation and had dedicated his life to uplifting the world around him. He was a kind of peaceful rebel-warrior who had been teaching meditation and breathwork since the 70's—whether the world was ready for it or not. Apparently, he had found his calling in his early teens. I appreciated that underdog spirit.

We eventually ended up purchasing the event tickets as a show of support, fully aware that we were not going to make it. We conveniently forgot about the event soon after.

But that day at work, somehow things started to effortlessly fall into place, and to my pleasant surprise, I had resolved the problem on hand far ahead of time. Whether by coincidence or not, my office was a short ride from Grand Central Station, and Gurudev Sri Sri Ravi Shankar's public talk was at the Waldorf Astoria—just a few city-blocks further north. And so that was that.

Jack of All Meets Master of All

An enthusiastic event volunteer greeted Alak and I as we entered the foyer of the iconic Art Deco style building on Park Avenue. I had previously been to several ostentatious Wall Street events at the Waldorf Astoria's finely appointed ballroom—a venue that has seen many presidents, singers, and celebrities on its stage.

The stage was well lit. Chairs were arranged neatly in a curvilinear pattern facing the stage. Like a diamond necklace around the neck of an elegantly dressed woman, the crystal chandelier hanging from the high ceiling added to the beauty of the room.

We took our seats. There was a comfortable-looking couch on the stage, which I presumed would be for the speaker of the event. A mic was placed next to the seat. A group of musicians seated on the right of the stage were tuning their instruments one last time. A simple arrangement of white flowers added to the otherwise spartan stage setup. The room was full. A lot of people seemed to know each other and were greeting one another with bear hugs and smiles. We felt a bit out of place.

The house lights dimmed before I could investigate who was in the crowd. A young, vivacious lady came up to the stage to open the event. Her demeanour was full of confidence, and she spoke eloquently about Sri Sri Ravi Shankar and the Art of Living Foundation he had established back in 1981.

'That's a pretty long time to stay with one thing. This guy must really love what he does,' I said in a snickering tone to my wife. A person sitting in front of us heard me and turned around to give me a disapproving look, as if I had just arrived from another planet and hadn't figured out what I should wear yet.

The introduction concluded promptly, and the musicians started playing a song. It was melodious and refreshingly different. The song, from the Kirtan genre of music, was quite a departure from the traditional kirtans I had grown up listening to. The lead singer strummed an acoustic guitar, and the fusion was soothing. It was a call-and-response style of music—the singer would deliver a line, and the audience would repeat it. Although I found it enjoyable, I couldn't get myself to sing along. I felt very awkward. The percussionist kept increasing the tempo and the song reached a crescendo. My eyes must have closed involuntarily.

Suddenly a loud cheer filled the room. The sound of arrhythmic clapping ricocheted off every wall. I slowly opened my eyes. Sri Sri Ravi Shankar walked onto the stage with a natural poise that I had never seen before. With his long hair and beard, he could have passed as a recluse, yet he seemed to be at home with everyone. He had the most serene smile on his face. Clad in a simple yet elegant white robe, he seemed to move like a cloud. He was clearly in some kind of joyful state.

He took a seat and gestured to the crowd to settle down as well.

'Hmmm?!'

Some people in the crowd started cheering at his simple interjection that came across as a mix of a question and wonder. I didn't quite get it.

'Illusion is an error of perception.' He began the talk. He had my attention at 'illusion'.

'Our experience of the world is based on perception. Since every perception is erroneous, the world is an illusion.'

The concept was certainly familiar, but it had a different appeal this time.

'Experiences are all of perception. The experiencer is the only reality. Look for the seer, the experiencer, in between experiences.'

There was a palpable feeling of warmth in his presence. His words were earnest but there was mischief in his tone.

His logic was sound, yet what he shared seemed to be beyond the purview of logic alone. Like an experienced parent guiding a child to think for themselves, he proceeded to drop breadcrumbs leading us in the right direction, rather than simply giving us a straight answer.

Sri Sri held the undivided attention of the crowd—including mine, to my own surprise—for the next twenty minutes or so. It was not his words that captivated me. It was something else. Perhaps it was his presence. Who was this person after all? Where had he been all this while? Had I been living under a rock? I was drifting away.

'Are you all really here? Are you listening? Now close your eyes and see who is listening. Who is questioning? Who is confused? You may not get any answer, but that is fine. Never mind.' He threw his head up and laughed like a child. It was hard to dismiss that unrestrained expression of his. I felt that the joke was really on me.

'Too much of discussion and wisdom will be difficult to digest. Let us all meditate for some time.' He shifted gears while measuring up the crowd. He asked everyone to sit comfortably and easily, for the whole purpose of meditation is to transcend bodily consciousness.

I was not ready to deal with the floodgate of thoughts that opened every time I attempted to meditate.

'If you are not relaxed, meditation won't happen,' he said.

He then asked everyone to close their eyes and bring their hands in front of their face as if holding an imaginary soccer ball.

'Bring your attention to the space in-between your hands . . . Now slowly bring your hands down.'

I have no idea what happened after that. There were some more instructions from him, but I was somewhere else. I learned about those other instructions only later, when Alak shared her experience with me. Where were all those never-ending thoughts? I'm pretty sure I had fallen asleep. I had a lot of sleep to catch up on, after all.

I regained consciousness to the melodious sound of a chant he sang to conclude the meditation. The chant drifted through the atmosphere like the music of innocence, revealed then lost. There was a distinct feeling of relief that I was yearning for. It was like the way one feels after an annoying speck of dust is finally removed from one's eye.

The chandelier above brightened up, bathing the entire ballroom in a bright hue. And with that light, I quickly returned to my pre-meditation tendencies. I began to look around, trying to find out if people around me had a better experience than I did. My competitive trader instinct was at work here as well. Some had still not opened their eyes. Some looked relaxed. Some were smiling. And a few were still in an inanimate state with their heads hung. I began to sweep the auditorium with my gaze.

My scanning was interrupted. There he was! I suddenly spotted the man who had asked me to run out of the burning building. He was looking straight in my direction, as if waiting for me to see him.

'Did you know how long it was? You all meditated for twenty-two minutes,' Sri Sri said, while glancing at a small clock on the side table.

No way! The thought in my mind was accompanied by a collective gasp from the crowd.

On long, cross-country flights, I would be so jealous of people who would snore away peacefully in visibly awkward and uncomfortable postures, as if naturally high on melatonin shots. Let's say resting in a sitting posture just wasn't my thing. And today, I had been knocked out for over twenty minutes. This was a first for sure.

While I was recovering from my state of disbelief and trying to figure out what had really hit me, he took some questions from the audience. He was lathering every question generously with a mix of wisdom, wit, and humour, sometimes throwing it back at the crowd, creating more wonderment. I kept looking at that guy in the audience every now and then. I wanted to make sure I didn't lose him this time. A couple of times our eyes met, acknowledging that we would connect right after the session. Eventually, the session came to an end. The musicians played one more song and Sri Sri glided out of the hall, albeit at a much slower pace this time, as people had lined up along his path to speak with him.

We met Shubhra and her husband in the aisle on our way out. Alak enthusiastically spoke about the wonderful time she had and thanked them for the invitation. While I too had a good experience, I was not prepared to talk about it just yet. I wanted to understand it more. And at the back of my mind, I first wanted to catch hold of that mysterious fellow.

But when I glanced back in his direction, he was gone. Furious at losing sight of him, I excused myself from the ongoing conversation and made my way out of the ballroom. I couldn't quite fathom how I had managed to lose him.

I wandered the halls of the Waldorf away from the venue and the crowds. My mind was full of all sorts of thoughts, interspersed with the memories of the time when I first met the mysterious stranger. Then, towards the end of the vestibule, I noticed him. Eyes locked on my target, I quickly made my way over to him. He looked at me with a confident smile, as though he had been expecting my arrival.

'Hi, I'm Kushal. Do you remember me?'

'Of course! I haven't forgotten a thing from that morning. I'm Banka.' A strange name for an Indian face, I thought.

I didn't know how to express my gratitude towards him. My awkwardness slowly melted away in silence.

'I was really hoping I'd meet you someday.' I said.

There was a sense of calm about him that I connected with immediately. Usually in such instances, deeply unprofound matters like weather and traffic lead the conversation. Fortunately, today we had something more to talk about.

'Did you enjoy the talk?' he asked, bringing me from the past to the current moment.

'Yes of course, it was very nice. My first-time meeting Sri Sri.'

'Same here. I felt like I instantly connected with him,' he said.

'He is definitely different from my impression of gurus. Can't really put my finger on what it is though.' I said, trying to be as politically correct as I could.

'His vibe, I guess.'

Sri Sri did have an unmistakably calm and friendly vibe.

'I would love to meet him. He comes across as someone who would have answers to all of my existential questions.' Banka said as he gazed in the direction of the ballroom.

Our brief conversation was interrupted by my ringing cell phone. It was Alak. I needed to make my way back to the hall, yet I didn't want to leave the conversation with Banka.

'I see you have to get going,' Banka smiled. 'Let's stay in touch.' I agreed immediately, relieved that the desire to continue our discussion was not one-sided.

In a near-jog back towards the venue, my mind was unusually still. It didn't take me long to find Alak. Our new friends came over to say goodbye. On the way out, they invited Alak and me to a SKY Breath Meditation Program. I didn't commit. It almost felt as if things were progressing all too fast on the first date.

We reached home, but I had not yet left the Waldorf. I kept replaying the exact sequence of events in my head for the next couple of days.

The Offer I Couldn't Refuse

In the middle of being screamed at during an intense trading session on a typical Wall Street afternoon, my cell phone rang.

It was Amit. I had met him for the first time at the Waldorf Astoria, the same afternoon I first saw Sri Sri. Shubhra had introduced him as her perfect half. A stick figure with a beaming smile and a corny sense of humour is all I could remember about him then. After that session, we had kept in touch. Later that summer, he had invited Alak and me to a white-water rafting trip on the Delaware River with a group of meditators. Initially, I had resisted and searched for an excuse. And finally, I had given in.

The adrenaline rush of rowing through white-water rapids with a bunch of calm groupies was a new flavour of contrast that I got to experience on that trip. Like a Jedi speaking with a young Padawan, they all took their time and spoke to me about why I should have learned the Sudarshan Kriya (SKY) breathing technique. None of them knew about my background. Were my inner feelings so evident? They all came across as part innocent, part well-meaning, and part pushy. All of them, without exception, were poor salesmen, and I found that strangely endearing.

Amit sounded caring and formal at the same time. I wanted him to tell him that he couldn't have picked a worse time to call, but that would have been rude. So, I kept my responses short and monosyllabic.

'I'm teaching the SKY breath technique from next Wednesday. And I want you to be a part of it,' said the soft voice on the other end of the line. Ever since I had first met him, Amit had kept inviting me to attend meditation workshops where they taught SKY breath. He was relentless. I was preoccupied. And so, each time I managed to come up with a convincing work-related excuse.

'I will check with Alak and get back to you,' I said.

'I just talked to her, and she said she will join if you're ready.' I could almost picture him with a big 'Gotcha' smile.

There was no escape this time. I said 'OK.'

I had no idea what to expect of the SKY Breathe Meditation program. Back then, some referred to it as the basic program. At least the name indicated that it was for beginners, but that was about it.

While a part of me was convinced this would soon end up becoming one more item on the list of things I had experimented with and dropped, somewhere I was hoping for a repeat of the experience I had that evening at the Waldorf Astoria.

On my way home, I called Banka.

Choiceless Unawareness

Banka's phone kept ringing.

I've met many people in my life thus far. Most are just fleeting encounters. Some I've known for so many years that they have become like the pictures hanging on the wall of my family home—a permanent fixture. But even after all this time, I wonder how many of them really know me. Not who they think I am, but the real me. It's interesting how you can know people for so long on a superficial level, yet sometimes, you meet someone who instantly gets you. Just like that.

Banka was one of those people. Every time we talked, the conversation led to deeper questions about life. Our conversations were to the point and direct. There was no mincing of words. Neither of us subscribed to the social norm of political correctness—at least, not with each other. We had hit it off. And surprisingly, I was comfortable letting my guard down around him.

He finally answered his phone.

'I just signed up for your program where you pay to learn how to breathe!' My words dripped with sarcasm. 'And I don't think I will go.' I blurted this out without wasting any time on customary greetings. There. The weight on my chest had lifted.

Banka did not waste any time either. He was not in the mood to entertain my life crises triggered by a snowballing workload. His usually calm voice suddenly became firm as he talked about the importance of managing my mind. He insisted that this practice could help me in every part of my life. I didn't give in.

'Just do it. Opportunities like these don't take reservations.'

I imagined a lion pouncing on a sneaky warthog.

From the beginning, he was a poster child for the importance of meditation. He reminded me of a hard-core advocate who distributes pamphlets outside the subway station. Why, I had no idea. But he was annoyingly adamant about it. His arguments were logical and sharp—like those of a highly educated state prosecutor. What annoyed me wasn't that he was simply ignoring my arguments—it was that he was right. He knew it, and so did I.

I made one last attempt to get out of it. 'Will you also go for the workshop?'

'I have to, if you are. Let's do it.'

I guess I had no choice. My mind floated back to the failed attempts I had made over the last few years to plug the gaping hole inside. The search for calling and purpose had taken me the world over, yet I was nowhere close to an acceptable answer.

I convinced myself that it couldn't hurt to try one more thing. Anyway, I was quite familiar with how the cookie usually crumbled.

A Glimpse of SKY

The program began with eight of us in tow.

There were some obvious, awkward, and profound moments during the first session of the program. I did feel a bit out of place, but Amit's affable personality eased everyone right in. Gentle yoga and breath work felt really good after a long day of work. All this was interspersed with some simple, yet thought-provoking, knowledge. Though it appeared obvious at surface level, implementing and living it truthfully could perhaps take a lifetime of uphill effort.

The difficulty level of the program was increasing too slowly. I began to wonder what I would run out of first— patience or breath.

The instructor would now and then ask us to 'sit comfortably and easily'. But I struggled to find comfort and ease after a point. Sitting on a yoga mat with a straight spine for an extended duration just wasn't my thing.

Amit shared how our existence consists of seven layers. Body, breath, mind, memory, intellect, ego, and the Self. He promised that we'd meet and greet each of these layers over the duration of the program. I wondered if there was a shortcut to skip the first six and get straight to the Self. Show me the Self!

Then arrived the big moment. We were going to learn the celebrated Sudarshan Kriya or SKY. By now, I had done my research and read all I could find on the internet about it. The only thing that I could gather about this secretive yogic breathing technique was that it had been introduced by Sri Sri Ravi Shankar. I had read all the scientific research validating it. But I still had no idea what it entailed, and so I was curious going in. Yet, on some level, I was quite sure that once I had experienced it, I would quickly lose interest. After all, that is who I was.

'*Su* is proper, *Darshan* is vision and *Kriya* is a purifying action. It is through the action of our own breath, we get the vision of who we are.' The instructor started with this brief introduction. After a succinct introduction, Sri Sri's mellifluous voice on a tape took over, and he started guiding us through the process.

Initially, it felt as if the floodgates of random thoughts had been opened. My mind was full of reflections that I had not entertained in the longest time. I was surprised at how some distant memories, some not-so-pleasant experiences from the past, and even sweet nostalgia flooded my awareness. Sudden flashes from that fateful morning in September came rushing in as if they had been waiting backstage for their time in the spotlight. It was undeniable and painful. For over three years, I had kept pushing those thoughts aside, distracting myself with the next thing as soon as the thoughts even attempted to cross my mind. This time there was no escape.

And then, just like the Millennium Falcon in Star Wars disappears into deep, dark space after going into hyper-drive, I slipped into nothingness. It was a different kind of void. There was nothing there, and yet it felt so complete.

It seemed as if I had lost complete awareness. Time had come to a standstill. I do remember hearing some instructions here and there. But it felt as if I was in an alternate reality or a parallel universe. It was something I had never experienced before. It felt as if I had dived from the surface of a choppy sea to the serene depth of a vast blue ocean. That space deep down below was devoid of even a faint ripple. I had no idea how long I sat at the bottom of this ocean. There was not a sound, not a thing around me.

As the process concluded, I very gently opened my eyes. They were moist. I felt light as a feather, cleansed by my own breath. SKY turned out to be so simple and enjoyable.

The feeling of deep rest was evident. I quickly checked my watch to make sure I hadn't pulled a Rip Van Winkle, who had slept silently for twenty years and missed the entire American Revolution. Barely an hour had passed.

I had a lot of questions I wanted to ask. Did I fall asleep? I did remember hearing all the instructions. What had just happened? Where did all those thoughts come from? And where did they vanish to? Had I succumbed to physical fatigue or was I meditating? My mind was racing to map this experience to all the things I had read about. But I couldn't speak. Perhaps I didn't want to ruin the silence that I was feeling inside.

With my eyes closed, I thought of my last conversation with Banka. I quietly thanked him in my head for twisting my arm to be a part of this. In that moment, I knew I had to listen to him more and more going forward, instead of listening to my questioning intellect.

As we walked back home that evening, I still wasn't sure what had knocked me over. Alak was excited to share her experience and hear mine. But I was not ready to talk. It was as if a wound up and tired workaholic went rafting in a river of calm. I continued to savour the experience while desperately wanting to return to that state. It was the same state I had experienced momentarily after the meditation in the Waldorf.

I think, for the first time in my adult life, I had consciously experienced the present moment with awareness. Of course, scores of books and blogs are awash with what it is to be in the moment and how one feels joy and love in that space, but only now did I realize how incredibly incomplete they all are in conveying the experience. After all, how do you communicate the thrill of navigating rapids to someone who has never tried river rafting?

That said, I was not ready to call it a day just yet. My Wall-Street-trained compulsive brain still had to do its homework and make sure this was not just beginner's luck.

Ready. Steady. Bang.

The enthusiasm and adrenaline rush of shooting past the starting line creates a distorted reality, in which the effort required to run a race suddenly appears trivial, and the finish line seems all too within reach. The first mile is always the fastest for an amateur running a marathon.

On the last day of the workshop, Amit shared how to practice SKY breath at home. A small, daily time commitment was all he asked for. It was the 'daily' clause in this non-binding verbal agreement that troubled me. Nevertheless, I threw my hat in the ring by raising my hand tentatively.

And that's how it began. I started strong right out of the gate, with full awareness that consistency had never been my strong suit. But I had Banka on my side who would keep me honest. I often felt that he had his gaze on me, like a hunter eyes an animal about to emerge from its den and run. I felt supported and intimidated at the same time.

A couple of weeks passed by without me missing a day. The Kriya was intriguing. Every day, it would harvest a different experience. The only predictable aspect was how, towards the end of the breathing, it would carry my mind to a thoughtless state and airdrop it there. I would continue to sit with my eyes closed, and when I opened them, more than twenty minutes would have gone by. This was a deep contrast from my earlier attempts at meditation, where I would sit for what felt like an eternity, only to realize that barely five minutes had passed on the clock. Despite the apparent upside of the practice, I was still certain that I would give it up once my initial enthusiasm was lost.

Was I meditating? Was I falling asleep? I had no idea. And at this stage, I couldn't tell the difference. What the heck, it felt good. And practicing it with Alak made it feel like we were on a little adventure together.

Indian summers are notorious. During summer vacations, I would ride my little bike outside all day and come home in the peak of a scorching afternoon to cool down. 'Are you topped up now?' My mother would ask as I gulped down gallons of cold water. I loved that feeling.

I would practice SKY in the morning, and the feeling of euphoria would evaporate by mid-day thanks to the daily grind of life and work. And by the next day, I'd be ready for it again. I would keep coming back to SKY, just for those moments of calm and stillness, which felt like ice water on a blazing summer afternoon. I had started looking forward to it.

But my mind continued to ask questions. I mean, apart from a few hours of calm, did this practice offer any demonstrable benefits? On the surface, it didn't seem like I had changed much at all. Once I asked Alak if she saw any change in me. 'What is it that you are looking to change?' she exclaimed. It was a somewhat adulatory response, but the matter rested there.

One day I experienced my own 'Aha!' moment. That day, some unpredicted movement in the financial markets caught everybody off guard at the trading desk at the investment management company I was working for. Panic erupted as we found out that the directional bets we had made did not go as planned. By now, I was quite used to such mayhem. It usually consisted of banging phone receivers, screaming at the top of your lungs, throwing your arms in the air, and swearing that would put a sailor to shame.

After all, when things don't go as expected, one always wants something or someone to blame. A phenomenon much too common on Wall Street. But that day, the stakes were much higher than usual. The panic was palpable.

I too would usually join this man-made faux crisis and participate wholeheartedly in the theatrics. But that day it played out differently.

For whatever reason, the madness around me didn't throw me off balance. I was both in the action—helping to resolve the issue at hand—and a witness—watching the sequence of events unfolding in front of me. In all this, I found no need to bang the phone receiver, scream, throw my arms in the air or swear like a sailor. Eventually, the storm passed like it usually does. I had managed to handle the entire situation in such a sterile and unanimated way that it had shocked me and my colleagues alike.

'Experiences are all of perception. The experiencer is the only reality. Look for the seer, the experiencer, in between experiences.' I was imagining Sri Sri's words from the Waldorf scrolling on the ticker-tape on the screen where stock prices usually flash incessantly.

Had I just been in touch with the experiencer? I felt like I had dipped my toes into the unknown. To know the unknown; is that all there is to be known? I was suddenly longing for a conversation with Banka.

Later that evening, over drinks, my boss came and asked me whether I was unwell or was smoking something—he was only half-joking. I laughed it off as he continued to probe what was going on. In reality, the only thing that had changed in my life was SKY. But I was not comfortable sharing that. I felt like Peter Parker who had just discovered his Spiderman powers of biological webbing. And yet, somewhere inside, I was not ready to come out for fear of being judged or mocked.

That evening, I had a silly smile on my face while walking home. It looked like this technique was doing something after all. Slowly but surely. However, the crawling pace of growth reminded me of my nosy aunt who would visit us when we were children. While we couldn't really tell the difference, every time she saw me and my sister, she only talked about how much we had grown since she last saw us—less than a year ago.

With every passing day, something was settling within. Slowly, like particles of dust after the mistral. I felt light and complete, as if my internal organs had been sifted through and eventually put back in place.

This was the year 2006. In context, this was still a few years before the first iPhone was launched. There were too many Starbucks joints compared to yoga studios in New York City. Though the winds of change were whispering, it was still the era where if you said the word 'meditation', others often heard it as 'medication'. It was considered a calling for either misfits or retirees. Somehow, my strait-laced, type-A profile didn't fit that stereotypical image. Against that backdrop, carrying the experience of SKY breathing back to the real world wasn't easy for me. I had created a block in my own mind that wouldn't let me share this little adventure with colleagues or friends.

I had once talked about this at length with Banka, who again dismissed me by reminding me that I care too much about what others think about me.

'Colour me curious, but do you really think you're so important that people have time to think about you all the time? Anyway, everyone is busy thinking about what others are thinking about themselves.'

As a typical sceptic, I would generally never accept anything at face value. But in a relatively short time period, there was a tangible experience. An experience I couldn't deny.

The runner had started strong.

Mile Marker Seven

When a runner crosses the seven-mile mark in a marathon, a mixed set of feelings begins to surface. There is a faint sense of achievement, but at the same time, the novelty of the race starts to lose its sheen—fatigue sets in, and along with it, a dash of boredom. Their attention drifts to the audience watching the race.

The days flew by swiftly. I had now been meditating for nearly two years. The honeymoon period was over. It felt as if I had crossed the seven-mile mark in my so-called spiritual journey. I was just about at the point where one has studied and practiced enough to be dangerous. Vanity set in. I was neither here nor there, but for some reason, it felt as if I had arrived. Knowingly or unknowingly, I gave myself permission to take the high road. I began judging others who were not on the same path. Suddenly, the friends who didn't meditate appeared to have made the wrong choices in life. I started making a disproportionately massive deal about the energy of people around me, and of the places where I spent time.

When something good happened, I struggled to mask the excitement and appear equanimous. After all, that's what established Yogis naturally do. On the contrary, if something bad happened, I blamed it on Karma. I found myself using the words 'bliss' and 'consciousness' way too much. If I remember correctly, my casual wardrobe had acquired an eastern influence, and a pair of metrosexual harem pants may have sneaked their way in. I may have even considered selling a kidney to buy Lululemon outfits in order to send the right external signals. I was curious about *mala* beads and healing crystals and seriously considered letting one appear around my neck or wrapped around my wrist. A new set of books was added to my bookshelf and some all-natural herbal supplements appeared in my travel bag. Any illnesses were attributed to the misalignment of the chakras. If that was not sufficient, I had embraced the word 'acceptance' as deeply as kale salads, wheatgrass shots, and disgusting green smoothies.

Some of these things happened naturally. Some I acquired through osmosis by being in the company of like-minded people, and a lot I steered clear of by observing the same like-minded people. There was no awakening anywhere in sight, but perhaps my *Kundalini* was being tickled. I was definitely tickled at the thought of it.

After 9/11, I couldn't find much joy in anything for long. Career, hobbies, travel destinations, food—everything seemed ephemeral and anything new quickly became old. Then came SKY, which was delightful, but now I was approaching a point where the excitement was fading away. I was yearning for change. I wondered if I was back to where I had started.

Pathologically or metaphorically, I was the undisputed emperor of boredom.

'Do you feel the same about brushing your teeth or taking shower every day?' Banka asked me.

'Sometimes.' I just said it to have the last word, though I didn't mean it.

It is said that routine and repetition are linchpins of any worthwhile pursuit. And I get that. You always row, row, row your boat, gently down the stream. Clearly, once doesn't cut it. In school, I had to write 'I will not talk in class again' a hundred times on the chalkboard. Once wasn't sufficient. Repetition perhaps turns something into a habit and makes it stick. But repetition doesn't create excitement; new experiences do. The mind gets so bored doing the same thing over and over again, that it simply gives up. Phrases like 'never again' or 'enough is enough' have been in the collective consciousness a lot longer than I have been on this planet.

I wondered if Sri Sri also got bored. After all, he had been at this for close to four decades now.

Wallflower in a Satsang

One afternoon, a friend called to ask me if I'd like to substitute for a guitarist who was unwell in a Kirtan band at a satsang. Say what? I declined. As politely as I could.

'Why didn't you agree?' Under the guise of this unassuming question, Banka was proposing that we at least go check it out.

I made a face as if he had offered me a slice of pizza with mouldy toppings.

I had agreed to many of Banka's requests and rather progressive thoughts, but this motion wasn't going to pass. At least, that's what I thought initially.

Satsang. A lot more goes on there than the name suggests—a space where like-minded people converge to sing, soak in knowledge, and meditate together.

While growing up, my mother would drag me to many satsangs. I would, later on, be compensated handsomely in ice cream for attending one, though that didn't reduce the

71

pain of going through it. Neither my experience, nor my outlook towards it, got better with time. My little sister and I would commiserate at these boring gatherings full of middle-aged men and women, clapping away and singing out of tune to even more boring music. Resistance from every cell of my body was futile. It was quite an ordeal for a ten-year-old to endure.

'Remember the one in the Waldorf with Gurudev? It wasn't anything like the satsang trauma from your childhood days.' Banka reinforced his case with heavy artillery.

The desire to experience that calm again and an opportunistic promise to go eat dosa afterwards pushed me closer to saying yes. It seemed that my satsang karma wasn't completely exhausted after all.

Driven by the idea that misery loves company, I reached out to a couple of my friends, reluctantly asking if they'd like to join us. No one agreed to come. The thought of sacrificing a Friday evening of fine wine, decadent food, and the company of good friends for a satsang must appear ludicrous, and I got the sense that perhaps a few of them questioned my mental state. I couldn't really blame them.

After a lot of hemming and hawing from my side, Alak and I finally made it to the event. It immediately hit me that this was a very different and informal setting compared to the Waldorf. It was an environment of extremes.

Men and women decked out in colourful Indian outfits and beautiful evening dresses were side-by-side with some wearing pants and t-shirts stained with the remnants of the day's meals. Students mixed with retirees. Veteran meditators and then those just checking things out, like me. Age, race, gender and religion appeared irrelevant here. My observation was interrupted by a bulky middle-aged woman who rushed past me and, with a sigh of relief, threw herself into the seat next to me so gracelessly that I felt a breeze. I was beyond uncomfortable. I wanted to leave, but Alak talked me out of it.

'We are here now. Let's stay,' she said resolutely. Eyebrows curled inwards, I slumped back into my seat like a defeated child. I felt as if Banka had already tipped her off to my brewing internal conflict.

An ensemble of musicians was set up on the low stage, which was decorated in white.

The meditation hall was filling up quickly as the time to start ticked closer. The sound of a guitar being tuned was replaced by a series of chords, followed by the baritone voice of the singer. The loud hum of the room immediately began to quieten down. The kirtans began in the familiar call-and-response style.

First kirtan. Second kirtan. Third kirtan. The energy in the room was ramping up in lockstep with the chatter in my mind.

'Why aren't you singing along?' Banka whispered in my ear, as if he was reading my mind.

'You have drunk the Kool-Aid. I haven't. This is not my type of music.' I rolled my eyes and lifted my shoulders in silent protest. At the back of my mind, I was imagining exactly how my friends from my amateur undergrad band would ridicule me if they found out that their guitarist had defected to singing kirtans.

'Just close your eyes and let go. Sing like nobody's listening. You still worry too much about what others think.' I didn't like that he saw right through me.

I looked around. There was a lady who was singing at the top of her lungs with her hands raised. Her malas were bouncing up and down with the movement of her body. Another man was clapping so hard that his wrists could have fallen off. Some were just sitting with their eyes closed, either meditating or sleeping. Most were singing their hearts out. One man was even smiling with his eyes closed as if he was having an out-of-body experience. Weird. Some in the back row were dancing. Their enthusiasm was encouraging the percussionist, who kept driving the tempo up. Even Alak seemed to be having a meditative experience. Perhaps I was the only misfit here.

Helpless and bored, I decided to take the plunge. Correction, not a plunge—I just decided to wet my toes. I closed my eyes and murmured one line in a way that even

I could barely hear. Suddenly, the entire room burst into a roar of laughter. All my friends, my family, my cousins, and their mothers-in-law appeared to be rolling on the floor in hysterical laughter, pointing their fingers at me. I couldn't really tell if they were laughing at my half-hearted effort, my singing, my apparent discomfort, or simply at the sight of what had become of me. I immediately opened my eyes. Nobody was there.

'This is not me. This is very different.' I told Banka with the awkwardness of a vegan monk at a steakhouse. 'Look at that guy with the camera streaming this live. I don't want anyone to tag me on Facebook.' I fully regretted agreeing to come here. Dosa suddenly appeared to be too little a reward to make up for the damage if word got out that I spent my Friday evenings attending these hippie love-ins.

'First they laugh at you. Then they wish they were you. Then they join you.' He paraphrased Gandhi's quote with the conviction of Churchill. He knew exactly what I was thinking.

'Come out of the reservoir of self-absorption that you are submerged in, and maybe just sit with your eyes closed. And then if you feel like doing so, repeat a line or two of the song. Just let go. I know letting go is difficult for you but trust me and just try.'

I was annoyed and helpless. To escape that room, I closed my eyes. It was just the two of us now—me and my existential conflict. My ego was screaming at the top of its lungs to hit eject and get the hell out of there. But my heart wanted to trust Banka's words.

The kirtans usually start mellow and slowly build up to a crescendo. As they go into hyperdrive, the crowd loses itself in the moment, becoming one with the music. I was sitting with my eyes closed as one of the Shiva Kirtans was approaching its crescendo. The drummer was engrossed in his music. The crowd was going bonkers. I was fairly certain that nobody would hear me sing in that noise. I started humming gently. From the corner of my eye, I checked again. Nobody even bothered to look at me. I began to sing along. I didn't understand the complete meaning of the words, but I kept on going.

It seemed to get a little easier. At least, I was no longer struggling with the words. A kirtan usually has just a handful of words that one sings repeatedly. It seems like it should get predictable and boring, but it doesn't. My chattering, irritated mind was beginning to calm. Have you ever tried crying loudly alongside a crying toddler? Suddenly when you cry, they go quiet. This felt something like that. As the sound of the music outside became louder than the noise inside, my mind was forced to rest. Later, I learned that the sounds enunciated in kirtans have been in the collective consciousness for thousands of years, and they carry subtle intentions to quieten the mind. Whatever.

The kirtan ended. There was a multi-second pause before the next one. The silence appeared beautiful. My mind was still. The pulsing of the music was slowly replaced by nothingness. It was the kind of silence you experience when you dive deep into a swimming pool. The feeling transported me to the session at the Waldorf. It had a comparable energy. Time stood still. I had never experienced such a contrast between sound and silence before.

That pulsating silence was delicate like a fresh snowflake. I wanted it to persist outside as well as inside my mind. However, an eager musician threw a pebble on the still surface of the lake with a strum of his guitar. Another kirtan was on its way. This time, the singer was off-key—like a needle scratching across a record. I prayed for more patience. Each minute felt like an eternity as this musical abomination continued. For whatever reason, the rest of the room didn't seem to mind. Even Alak was smiling with what appeared to be some expression of contentment.

'Perhaps this is what acceptance feels like.' Banka tried to ease my annoyance. That guy always had a wisecrack for me at just the right moment.

Despite my irritation, I did notice how my level of tolerance was beginning to shift, albeit too slowly for the human eye to notice. I wanted to call my mother and tell her I went to a satsang. She would be happily surprised.

This experience broke my resistance towards Satsangs. I attended a few more over the next couple of months. Kirtans were surprisingly growing on me, terrible vocalists included. Listening to Bach's symphonies or Led Zeppelin's riffs with one's eyes closed transports one to a different space. Similarly, kirtans escorted me someplace else. Somewhere I hadn't been before with music. Without a complex harmonic language, kirtans appeared approachable, simple, and innocent—like a childhood friend.

Once I reached home after the satsang, I pulled out my guitar and tried my hand at some of the tunes that were stuck in my head.

As I dwell upon the evening of my first satsang, I recollect how the room was blanketed by a feeling of connectedness and ease at the same time. It was also the first time I had ever understood that the sublime could be only a step removed from the ridiculous.

A Silent Scream

By now, a few positive affirmations here and there had lent a gentle assurance that the seed of meditation had germinated. However, the green shoot had still not cut through the topsoil, and so my progress wasn't convincingly visible. My mind, like a fidgety toddler in a car seat, would ask the same annoying question every now and then: Are we there yet? Living in a city like New York only added more fuel to this fire that demanded instant gratification.

The usual madness of life continued at a frenetic pace, and time seemed indifferent to my overflowing list of priorities. Just then, an email arrived in my inbox, announcing a silent retreat with Sri Sri Ravi Shankar. He was coming to Philadelphia as part of his US tour.

The email said it was a detox for the body and mind. This description conjured up images of several expensive, new age detox routines I had tried in the past. Since then, I had developed an aversion to pretty much anything green, although it was a good workout for my gag reflex.

I had never voluntarily kept quiet for an extended period of time, so the challenge was intriguing. Moreover, by now, I had realized I was fighting a losing battle resisting it. Between Banka and Alak, the two walls closing in on me, I had nowhere to escape. Before I even realized it, I found myself in a car driving down to Philadelphia with Alak and a couple of friends. A spiritual double date of sorts.

It didn't take me long to realize that the universe and its co-conspirators had pushed me yet again into the deep end of the pool. When I learned about what silence really meant during the first few hours of the program, I was ready to leave immediately. No talking. No eye contact or gestures to anyone else. No reading. Or writing. Or listening to music. And the final nail in the coffin—no electronics. Just long hours of meditation. The panic on my face must have been evident. A middle-aged man wearing a volunteer's badge and sweatpants clearly meant for someone ten pounds lighter met my gaze with a Cheshire cat smile. To make matters worse, I had forgotten that we had driven here in someone else's car.

As someone who has been accused of having my phone attached to my head, the initial hours felt torturous—like an addict going through rehab. Those green juice detoxes were a piece of cake in comparison.

Just like the world appears saturated in a shade of pink when looking through rose-tinted glasses, my mind began finding faults with everything and everyone as if it had put on complaining glasses.

First, there were far too many people there for my taste. The meditations were long and painful. The breaks were short and the restroom lines long. It pushed my buttons every time a person stepped on my yoga mat, snored, or silently passed gas. Imagining this experience for three more days didn't bring any comfort.

The special Hollow and Empty meditations on the course are designed by Gurudev to lead one inward while scrubbing out negative past impressions. The only instruction was to sit absolutely still—like a statue—through the meditation. I could follow that instruction for just about a minute. After that, I began to move like a metronome. Adjusting for some pain here and accommodating for some twitch there. At some point, my back had started hurting as if two pebbles were being ground together with bits chipping off. I also developed a strange sensation in my left foot that was so uncomfortable I sincerely questioned what I was doing here. The never-ending guided meditations appeared to be a contemporary version of medieval torture. I couldn't decide what was more painful—the meditations or the blissful state of the people around me. Some of them genuinely seemed to be enjoying themselves. Perhaps I was desperate for an experience. An experience that just wasn't there.

Every meditation would end with a soothing chant. Although I didn't understand the meaning of it, nothing had ever felt so comforting. The persecution was finally over. I would quickly open my eyes, only to find a bunch of crazies with the most joyful smiles on their faces, as if they had knocked on heaven's door and someone had actually let them in.

During lunch hour, I devised a brilliant plan to stuff myself with extra food so that I could sleep through the agony of a meditation or two. But they ran out of food by the time it was my turn in the line. Furious, I returned to my yoga mat, being sure to step on everyone else's mat along the way. It was like all the forces in the universe had teamed up against me. My stomach let out an audible rumble, as though violating the hall's pin drop silence in protest.

I managed to silence my protesting body with a promise to head home after the session. I was done.

Renewing the Wow Factor

During the dinner break, I reached out to Banka, and informed him of my decision to drive back home. Needless to say, the self-appointed keeper of my moral compass wasn't too happy.

'Didn't really think you were the quitting type. But up to you.' He walked away, refusing to talk to me further.

I wrote a note on a piece of paper for my friend, requesting that he let me borrow his car for a couple of days. My plan was to drive back home that night and then return to Philadelphia to pick up the survivors of the silent retreat. I looked for him everywhere—including the bathrooms—but he was nowhere to be found. Finally, I returned to my spot—and there he was. The next session hadn't even started but the ultra-sincere, annoying overachiever was already sitting on his yoga mat with his eyes closed. I waited for him to open his eyes so I could submit my plea. And just then, the lights went dim. Sri Sri walked onto the stage.

I reluctantly took my seat. That evening, he spoke about commitment. He spoke about the doubting nature of the mind that was probably looking to run away from here. His words were full of wit and empathy. He promised it would get better with time. It felt as if he had read my note and was speaking directly to me. He wasn't trying to convince anyone, but there was conviction in his presence. I stayed.

When I first met him in New York, his wisdom and his sense of humour had appealed to my otherwise reluctant mind. This time, I experienced and enjoyed a lot more of that. Sometimes only he laughed at his own jokes, but the childlike innocence behind it came through clearly. And I was beginning to feel at ease with him.

People around me, including Banka, referred to him as Guruji or Gurudev. I continued to address him as Sri Sri.

Like the Patriots' twenty-five-point comeback in Super Bowl LI, by the third day of the program I was meditating like a warrior. The aches and pains in my body became somewhat tolerable. People no longer seemed as annoying. The lines for food became more manageable. My internal resistance had diffused. The final meditation almost felt like listening to poetry in the rain.

During the drive back home, I processed all that had happened over the past few days. My mind rattled with thoughts in an otherwise quiet car.

While at some level it appeared that I had suffered a great deal, the weekend workshop with Sri Sri was refreshing. It also reinforced the SKY practice that I had learned earlier. Similar to how April showers bring spring flowers, there was a palpable feeling of rejuvenation in my personal practice. The quality of the detox was different than anything I had expected; it was almost like drinking algae, kale and spirulina Green Goddess from a fire hose.

Ms Jain was my English tutor in high school. My primary schooling was in my mother tongue—Gujarati. Ms Jain's passion for the language combined with my father's persistence stoked my own love for it and got me into the habit of reading.

Somehow, just spending a few days with Sri Sri had a similar impact on my meditation practice. I started practicing SKY regularly—but this time not just to check a box in my daily routine. My mind no longer resisted it as something boring. It wasn't demanding a change of pace anymore. It was too early to say, but I might have broken my previous streak! Had I finally found something that did not bore me, or had my mind just fallen into a steady relationship with boredom? I guess only time would tell.

Like a Formula One race car with new tires, there was now a renewed sense of energy in the system for the same technique that had begun to wear thin.

Four-Letter Word

It's not the four-letter word you're thinking.

I was struggling with an internal resistance. Did I need a coach or tutor for this path that I had embarked upon? The main problem was that the word associated with such a coach is 'guru'. I grimaced at the thought of it.

The benefits of the SKY breath continued to accumulate at a steady pace. My existential questions still lurked, but the restlessness associated with it was losing its intensity. Subconsciously, a habit was forming.

As life continued to flow along with the river of time, I had questioned my education, my work, my journey, my relationships, my reasoning, my writing, and of course, myself. Now, life presented one more aspect for me to question—the need for a guru.

Call it a curse of Wall Street culture, where one was trained to never accept anything at face value. I could take huge bets in the financial market without blinking an eye. Almost all of the decisions in my life were evaluated by intellect. Perhaps, sprinting through the rat race had conditioned me to judge everything with the head, leaving the heart behind as a silent witness.

I appreciated the simplicity of the wisdom and knowledge that Gurudev shared. I really enjoyed reading his books. It was Einstein who once said, 'If you can't explain it simply, you don't understand it well enough.' During my college days, I would always rank my professors by how simply they could break down a concept. By now, I had already put Sri Sri Ravi Shankar under the same lens. I liked how he could deconstruct the most esoteric topic into a palatable form; easy to internalize and digest. One more box checked. But . . .

Perhaps my resistance towards gurus was the direct result of another type of conditioning—this time from my childhood days. The gurus I had come across while growing up in India had turned out to be either squarely unimpressive or mired in one scandal or another. Their teachings were deeply rooted in ritual and religion.

Some of these fraudulent personalities would garner large followings by preying on weak minds full of desires or helpless hearts seeking some relief. Even today, there is no dearth of such individuals who take advantage of people's faith.

Doubt and confusion seemed to be trusted companions on my spiritual path—especially with a living master leading the way. Even amidst the handful of people that followed Jesus, there was always one who doubted him. The uncertainty in my mind was growing like a colony of E. coli.

'Could you be any more confused?' Banka once asked. 'Perhaps you like to remain in that state of confusion so that you don't have to take responsibility for making lasting decisions.' I wanted to ignore him so hard that he doubted his own existence.

That said, most of my conversations with Alak were now about Gurudev and his wisdom. Unpacking and debating esoteric spiritual concepts with her had become my favourite pastime. She, from the very beginning, was a lot more open to the concept of a guru. And her conviction was strangely comforting in my moments of resistance or weakness. But I wouldn't admit it publicly—and definitely not in front of her.

One night, during our bedtime reading, Alak read a beautiful story about Buddha to me.

Once during his travels, Buddha passed by the village of Kesaputta. A group of innocent villagers came to meet the enlightened one and expressed their confusion about which philosophy to subscribe to. It so happened that many saints passed by that village, and each talked about their own teachings, philosophies, and techniques. Often, one's school of thought would contradict that of another.

This was some 2,500 years ago, but it still feels so relevant. The same human mind and the same problems, I thought.

The Buddha simply told them that they had a right to be confused! Just hearing that felt like a validation of my own confusion.

He then selflessly advised the villagers not to trust anything simply because it had been passed down through tradition—not because the elders said so, nor because it is prescribed in some scripture. This was equally applicable to what he was saying as well.

'Only if you have seen it and experienced it for yourself to be right and true, then you accept it.' Buddha concluded.

I was cautiously optimistic, but in a strange way. Cautious about following a guru, and yet optimistic as deep within me, Gurudev felt different. He definitely didn't fit the mould of the stereotypical guru I held in my mind.

Of course, optimism is like a wheelbarrow. Nothing happens until one really starts to push. So, I kept chugging along.

It left me vulnerable—opening doors that I had managed to keep shut all this while. I felt a distinct lack of control.

'Drop the prejudice. Let your experience alone guide you,' said Banka. Like Morpheus in *The Matrix*, he was asking me to make a choice.

I could take the blue pill, and evaluate this entire Path—the practice, the master, and the community—through intellect alone. If I did that, I'd likely dash out of the circus.

Or I could take the red pill and descend from my head to my heart—and then see how deep the rabbit hole continued.

III

The Path Itself Is the Teacher

It is said that the spiritual path is really short.
Just 12 inches.* From head to heart.

* Not drawn to scale. For it may take lifetime(s) to walk it.

Monk'i Mind

To move forward in life, one must use the mind.
To move inwards, however, one must drop the mind.

What do you do when you feel you are stuck in life? Stuck in the quicksand? The more you try to get out, the deeper you sink. So, what do you do? You strategize, you plan . . . but nothing works.

If life were a Pac-Man game with seven levels, I was stuck at level three. Despite all my efforts, I was unable to convincingly move past my mind.

With a few years of SKY breathing under my belt, I was now aware of the stubborn tendencies of my predictably irrational mind. Of the way it liked to jump around between the future and the past. How it focused on the feeling of lack. How it did the exact opposite of what I wanted it to do. But with all that awareness, there was still one problem: I struggled to overcome it.

I was the yellow Pac-Man of my own life. Running around to get this and that, being chased and snubbed every now and then by the colourful ghost—my own mind.

For time immemorial, seekers and philosophers have tried to win over the mind and achieve a state of 'no-mind'. Mushin, a Zen expression, refers to the 'mind without mind'—a mind not occupied by thoughts or emotions.

In my spiritual shopping days of the past, I had dabbled in different theories and approaches that claimed to help achieve a state of no-mind.

One approach prescribed focusing on a sense-object. For example, a calming sound or a ray of light. It is said that with sincere concentration, one can weed out unwanted thoughts.

I tried, but it didn't work.

Another popular approach—now known as mindfulness—encourages one to be aware of the experience of the senses. Becoming aware of your own state of mind through your own thoughts and emotions is being mindful. Once you notice your mind drifting, you consciously bring it back into the present moment.

Sounds easy, but it was too much work.

While I couldn't quite get there, I did notice that all of these approaches had one thing in common. Effort.

They were all frontal cortex activities. They all required some form of work—concentrating on something or not thinking about anything. They appealed to my logical mind, but they did not help me escape it.

The yellow Pac-Man was now searching for that magic pellet, with which he could neutralize the ghosts and make them retreat for a while.

And then I was introduced to Sahaj Samadhi Meditation. The word Sahaj means effortless.

The program began with the instructor offering a little prayer of thanks to all the masters of the past, who managed to keep this wisdom alive by passing it on from generation to generation. It was very soothing, and on some level, it felt very familiar. Suddenly, it seemed as if the entire room was filled with pulsating ethereal energy. The faint fragrance of sandalwood from the incense stick was quite pleasing. Immediately after that, all of us were sent out of the room and one by one, were invited back inside. My turn came. I was clueless about what to expect. The teacher whispered a simple monosyllabic sound to me. She said this was my mantra.

Like most things in life, Sahaj turned out to be something unexpected. It was an innocent technique to dive deep within oneself. Or something like that. It elevated the quality of my meditations. I couldn't fathom how it worked. But it did.

There was a time when I would sit down to meditate for what—thanks to a barrage of thoughts—felt like an eternity, but barely five minutes would have passed. But now, the mantra helped turn that pattern on its head. Using my mantra, I could disappear somewhere and return after what felt like five minutes, but more than twenty minutes would have passed on the clock.

The mantra would cut off the repetitive and connected thoughts in my reeling mind.

Many forms of meditation involve focusing solely on the breath or an object. As the mind wanders, which it almost always does, the poor meditator often moves to daydreaming. I too struggled with this in the past. But this mantra-based meditation technique was different. It automatically stopped the stream of thoughts, and I could ease into a meditative state.

Sahaj taught me the importance of the balance between effort and effortlessness. The gentle effort to bring the mantra into the awareness, and then simply letting go. It worked like a charm. The combination of SKY breathwork and Sahaj became the avocado toast of my daily practice.

The mysterious mantra can never be shared with anyone. It is like sowing the seed of meditation and covering it with the soil on top.

Our mantras are the only secrets Alak and I still keep from each other.

Red and Yellow Yoga Mats

Effort is the key in the relative,
Effortlessness is the key to the Absolute.

—Gurudev

'Get your car cleaned up. You'll be driving Gurudev to the hotel.' The communication was delivered to me with the gravity of a top-secret navy seal mission. The person was perhaps expecting me to do a happy dance, but I was still recovering from the events leading up to this moment.

It all started when I heard that Gurudev was coming to New Jersey for a Meditation and Yoga event. This mass meditation was organized at the enormous NJ Convention and Expo Centre. The lead organizer in charge of the event reached out, asking me if I'd like to volunteer my time. It was a slow summer at work. I figured I had nothing to lose, so I threw my name in the hat. I was put in charge of audio and video production for the event. Easy, I thought.

The first time I went to see the venue, I realized what I had really signed up for. The space was more appropriate for large car shows and exhibits, not for a meditation event. Sound was bouncing off the forty-foot-high ceilings, shiny un-carpeted cement floors, and distant walls—creating an annoying echo. My heart skipped a beat.

That day in the volunteer meeting, I brought up this potential issue, but no one really seemed to understand its gravity. The logistics team's singular focus was food for the 5,000 participants. In that moment, I felt like even if I fell into a lake full of piranhas, nobody would hear my cry for help.

The following week, I went in with a team of professional sound engineers, who unanimously agreed that we had picked the worst possible venue from an acoustics point of view. They promised to 'try their best' to mitigate the issue. I remained far from convinced.

T minus 1 day. I had followed every single recommendation from the sound engineers. Curtains were hung from the ceiling to avoid sound reflection. Array speakers were installed at certain intervals with a programmed delay to account for the time taken for sound to travel to the end of the room and back. The stage was moved twice as part of this hustle. Despite all this, there was a noticeable echo in the room. And it kept getting worse towards the back of the room. I was out of options. I had tried every single option available. And I had failed. I felt terrible to have let everyone down.

I left the venue in despair that night. The next day, Gurudev would lead over 5,000 people in a series of guided meditations in that space—provided they could hear him. I could imagine people complaining about the sound and asking for refunds. This was a ticking time bomb.

Unable to sleep, I reached out to Banka and told him everything.

'Let go.' Came the brief answer. 'You have done everything possible. Now just be.'

What? No way. That stuff is for the weak. I, and I alone, forge my own destiny through self-effort. I was struggling inside. Of letting go or hanging on, or letting go of hanging on, or hanging on to letting go.

'Tonight, when you sleep, feel that you have dropped everything and given everything to the universe—your body, your mind, your breath, your thoughts, your feelings, your environment—everything is offered to the Divine and you have nothing now. Have nothing and be nothing.' Banka reminded me of this piece of wisdom from Gurudev that we had read together once.

I didn't know exactly how to do it. But I closed my eyes and remembered Gurudev. I told him I had tried really hard. And I silently apologized. I meditated and fell asleep. My spinning head slowed down as the physical exhaustion took over.

The next day I reached the venue a little late. I was wandering around outside, avoiding people. The program inside had just started. Just then, Gary, a long-time meditator from Iowa and also one of the event leaders, came running towards me. I couldn't read his face.

I noticed some activity by the main entrance. People had started pouring out and there was noticeable movement by the door. I saw a volunteer running towards my car with a yellow cloth in his hands.

I had begun to notice a yellow ochre shade that was a constant backdrop wherever Gurudev was seated. Soon I realized that it was a piece of cloth that went everywhere with him. Just like blooms of marigold mark the arrival of spring, this shawl-like piece of cloth always arrived ahead of Gurudev.

Whether traveling in a car, train or plane, the mysterious piece of cloth would be a constant companion. However fine-looking the tapestry of the couch may be, there will always be this cloth on top. Later on, I learned it had a name too. Asana.

The Asana was now waiting on the seat next to me. Waiting for its rightful master to arrive.

Gary paused in his tracks. 'Great job with the sound man. You were making such a big deal about it!' He patted me and kept running in the direction he was headed. I ran inside the meditation hall. Light music was playing, and the sound was crystal clear. No echo whatsoever! What?!

I then noticed that the floor was covered with thousands of red and yellow yoga mats. That did it! It worked like a carpet and magically absorbed all the sound! It turned out someone had sponsored these beautiful yoga mats at the last moment, and I had no idea about it. They weren't yoga mats. They were life-saving devices. I was ecstatic. I teared up.

Universe—1. My worrying mind—0.

I was ready with my car. It was shining inside out as if I just picked it up from the dealership. Soon Gurudev would take the passenger seat. Only I hadn't had a chance to figure out the directions to his next stop. My concentration was repeatedly broken by the three passengers in the back seat. Eagerly awaiting Gurudev's arrival, their continuous laughter seemed to climb in sync with my anxiety level.

Gurudev walked out, turned around, and waved to the crowd. I looked around to make sure there were no other cars in the vicinity. He opened the door of the car. The door wouldn't open—it had auto-locked and none of us had noticed in the excitement. In a frenzied and uncoordinated move, both my hands reached for the dashboard and pressed all the buttons possible. The door clicked. He casually opened the door and jumped in the car as if nothing had happened. Phew. I didn't really know what to say. I uttered something profound—'Hi Gurudev!' He smiled.

I started the car and slowly pulled away from the waving crowds. Gurudev seemed to be at home with us. The passengers in the back seat were quiet for the first time in the last hour.

Not knowing what else to say, I began introducing everyone, thinking it would be so cool if he addressed me by my name.

'By the way, I'm Kushal and she is . . .' I began introducing all the passengers in the back seat.

'Yes, I know, I know.' He interrupted softly. 'We met the day you all did your first Sudarshan Kriya.'

He said this so casually. He looked straight into my eyes. Nodded with a big smile and a blink. He then turned around, closed his eyes, and dissolved into meditation. The car vibrated with his presence. I kept looking at him. Luckily, there was no backseat driving from Alak that day. As we came to the end of the drive, he came out of the meditation, and talked to each one of us in the car, answering questions. I had no questions to ask but I asked for a hug. I felt silly. I should have waited at least until we were out of the car.

We made it to the hotel where he would be leading a satsang at a silent retreat. Volunteers were already waiting to receive him. He didn't step out immediately. He waited for me. I parked the car and walked to the other side. He then stepped out. He embraced me in a warm hug. For a moment, I lost my sense of where and who I was.

He moved on. Everything around seemed to be moving in slow motion. I was happy. Where were the thoughts that rose and fell like cosine waves? Perhaps the universe had silently stepped in and laid red and yellow yoga mats in the empty space between my ears.

False Sense of Control

What do all of these things have in common?
How others feel . . .
The past . . .
Time lost . . .
Weather . . .
Traffic . . .
Life . . .

'Cessna niner-three-zero-zero foxtrot cleared for take-off on runway two-two. Maintain two thousand feet after the climb.' The Air Traffic Controller's instructions came through the headset, muffled by static noise.

It was a clear and chilly January morning at the Essex County Caldwell Airport in New Jersey. The aircraft slowly crawled and aligned on the runway before coming to a stop.

'Flight path, check. Flaps zero. Ailerons into the wind. Oil temperature and pressure, check. Power and instruments, check.' I closed my eyes for a second and took a deep breath in. It was time.

I opened the throttle fully. A little pressure on the left rudder. The plane started to roll with all its might.

My first solo flight. There was no turning back from here. I looked to my right. The usual guiding voice of my instructor wasn't there. I was on my own. I was still on the ground, but the butterflies in my stomach had already taken off.

'Air speed alive. Thirty knots. Forty knots. Fifty knots. Lift off!'

And just like that I was airborne. The initial feeling of nervousness was taken over by the indescribable feeling of freedom and exhilaration. The aircraft stabilized at 2,000 feet, and my mind was no longer intensely checking the cockpit instruments. A stream of thoughts poured in, as if waiting for the slightest opening to emerge.

At one level, I appeared to be in full control of the aircraft. I was completely aware of every lever, every gauge and the aerodynamic impact of the slightest movement. But from another point of view, nothing seemed to be in my hands. Even the faintest gust of wind was enough to rattle everything. Smaller planes are as sensitive to wind as a thin scrap of paper. I felt a pit form in my stomach.

A disciple was once pouring his heart out in front of his master.

'What are you afraid of?' asked the master to his student.

'I am afraid of losing control,' he said.

'Well, you just lost all the control to fear,' Replied the master.

Most people have a deep need for a sense of control. Having earned the title of a 'control freak' from a young age, I definitely have that tendency. But is it really control that I seek, or is it just the sense of control?

I have often tried to solve the mystery of how much of life is free will, and how much is deterministic. Am I really in full control of my life, or am I just like a fish in an aquarium that seemingly swims around at will, but who's confines are firmly defined?

I studied what I wanted to, chose the profession I liked, and chose my own life partner. That suggests I'm in full control. Or was it instead that at every crossroad in life, circumstances arranged themselves in such a way that I had no choice but to make the decisions I made?

If I'm not the one in control, then who is? And if everything is out of control, then is there even any point in self-effort?

Just then, I passed over Route 80. I heeded this visual cue and adjusted the heading by turning right into the wind.

The giant freeway beneath was stretched out like a python. The cars, like little breadcrumbs, were moving in synchrony. Identical roofs of hundreds of homes were arranged neatly in well-planned grids—perfect squares and rectangles. It felt like I was staring at a screenshot of SimCity—a city-building simulation game. At the same time, behind this perceived organization lurked massive chaos. Imagine what must be going on in each head in each car or home. I didn't even want to know. Zoom in even more, and one would find molecules zapping about at random, following a Brownian motion with a drift. Such unbelievable chaos!

It's fascinating how both chaos and orderliness coexist so seamlessly. I can't even tell where one ends and the other begins.

Wait, why was I suddenly having such serious thoughts? Perhaps higher altitudes make people more thoughtful and inspire them to think of the big picture.

'Cessna niner-three-zero-zero foxtrot—inbound traffic reported at two o'clock. Maintain altitude.' The air traffic controller's cautionary squawk interrupted my chain of thoughts.

An airplane doesn't really experience a traffic jam in the air. But on the ground, it's different. Is it the same with our mind? Amidst daily life, the mind is filled with so much clutter. Yet, when it logs on to a different dimension—

often during meditation—it experiences a different level of peace and quiet. Little thought traffic.

By now, I had turned on final approach. The controller had cleared me to land. I was barely minutes away from touching down. The little tin bird was perfectly aligned with the runway. The buildings on the ground were growing larger as the aircraft continued to descend. A feeling of delight took over me as I saw the finish line.

I began thinking about the planes that did not land on 9/11. Not now. I needed to focus.

'Carburettor heat on. Fuel mix lean. Flaps down full. Speed sixty-five knots.'

Fifty feet. I pulled the power out and lifted the nose up slightly in the final manoeuvre. The speed at which the land was moving toward me suddenly increased. The landing markers on the runway passed beneath me, and gravity did the rest to ensure a smooth touch down.

The plane continued to roll down the runway, slowing down in sync with my heart rate. As the adrenaline began to subside, my mind swung back to my internal debate about a sense of control.

Once, at a public talk in Washington DC, Gurudev spoke about being in control.

'Wake up and see—are you really ever in control? What do you control? Perhaps a tiny part of your waking state! You can't even control the thoughts and emotions coming to you. You may choose to express them or not, but they come to you without your permission. Most of the functions of your body are not under your control. Do you think you are in control of all the events in your life, in the world, or in the universe? That is a joke!' He paused briefly.

'When you look at things from this angle, you need not be afraid of losing control, because you have none to lose,' Gurudev said with a gentle smile.

The plane came to a stop, but my mind continued to roll.

I Didn't Listen

If something doesn't feel right, it usually isn't.

Sometimes being in action gives an illusion of progress. Like how one keeps changing lanes in traffic only to realize that the change wasn't really helpful. And just like that, I began fixing things that were not broken.

After spending nearly a decade in the US, Alak and I were beginning to feel homesick. We both strongly felt the need to go back to where it all began. Perhaps the most commonly experienced, yet usually ignored, flavour of internal conflict for every immigrant. After much deliberation, we both agreed that it was time to wake up from the American dream.

We were feeling pretty good about all that we had managed to check off our *things-to-do-in-a-new-country* list. We had far exceeded our own expectations of ourselves.

If we indeed continued in this way, the future would bring more of the same. Besides, going back to India could also open a new chapter in our spiritual journey. We didn't think we were really compromising on anything. We both resolved to move back home—back to our roots.

Earlier that summer, Gurudev had once again visited New York. It was like a walk down the memory lane from five years ago. But this time I had made sure to keep my calendar open, because I wanted to be around him. I really had no specific agenda. I found out who was hosting him, and one afternoon, after a meditation session with some corporate CEOs, I followed Gurudev to where he was staying. I swiftly pulled my car out of the parking lot, gaining a three-minute head start on the others—a massive advantage when it comes to chasing the guru. Naturally, when we reached the place on the Upper East Side, there were only a couple of us there. And just like that, I once again found myself nearly alone in the room with him. The good old Asana was neatly placed in the centre of a massive couch by the window. He placed himself in the centre of the Asana. I was standing in a corner. He smiled and called me closer with a gesture.

'Haan? What do you want to ask?' He posed the question warmly. I was overjoyed to hear it again.

I walked up to him. I wasn't mentally prepared to ask anything.

'Guruji, I feel like moving back to India. Do you think it's a good idea?'

The question just came to me. Why? I have no idea. It wasn't like I had been waiting and planning to ask this question. I certainly wasn't asking for permission. I guess the thought was looming large in my mind and so it must have just popped out. I immediately felt stupid for asking such an inconsequential question. In the very next moment, I wanted him to tell me what I wanted to hear.

He smiled gently and closed his eyes for three seconds, which felt like an eternity. I had no idea what aspect of consciousness he tapped into during that time.

'Not now. After February.' He said with strong conviction.

Wait, what? Not now? Why? How was that even possible? Its July now. I had been offered a leadership role at a very prestigious firm, and Gurudev was asking me to wait eight months? Who in their right mind would keep the offer open for me for that long? I wanted to tell him all of that.

Before I could give him any context, people poured into the room and rushed to where he was seated. Alak was one of them. Right behind her was Banka. Alone and outnumbered, I stepped back.

How did you get here so fast? Alak asked me with her eyes. All this time, she was trying to decode the look on my face. Banka was smiling as if my anguish was giving him some kind of wicked pleasure.

My best laid plans had been dismantled by one unassuming answer. I didn't really think Gurudev understood the gravity of the matter. Should I listen to him and let go of this opportunity that I had worked so hard for? Or should I take a chance? What's the worst thing that could happen? I was now conflicted inside. I wanted to kick myself for opening my big mouth.

But why was I experiencing such a conflict within me? This was perhaps the first time I realized how much Gurudev's words meant to me. I would not have felt the way I did if anyone else had asked me to change my plans. But now I couldn't ignore the unsettled feeling inside me, even if I tried.

I had moved so far ahead in the planning, and now Gurudev had tossed a wrench in the works. I wanted to confirm if what I'd heard was right, but there was no one I could ask. Alak pushed me to ask him again, but that never happened.

Let's connect later, Banka gestured before disappearing from the scene.

Leap. No Faith.

Only thing in agreement with reality is your limited perception. After all, you create your own reality based on what you perceive,' said a voice to the frog in a well.

I reached out to Banka after coming home. I could barely make out what he was trying to say. His voice sounded so distant. I almost felt a strange sense of relief when I couldn't speak to him. But it wouldn't have taken Van Gogh's imagination to know what he was trying to tell me.

'Why don't you meditate and then call me back?' Banka said before hanging up. I'm sure he was picking up on the nervousness in my voice.

In that despondent state, wanting to share what I was feeling inside, I would have run two laps of Central Park if he had asked me to. So, I sat down to meditate without arguing. Of course, my meditation was flooded with thoughts. My body was stationary, but my mind was all over. I tried to pole vault past these thoughts with help of my mantra, but for some reason it didn't help. On a wobbly plateau at the end of my wits, a wild battle was raging between logic and something beyond logic.

I opened my eyes after twenty minutes that seemed like an eternity. The phone rang. How does he always know the exact moment when my meditation ends? Uncanny.

I narrated the entire incident to him in almost one breath. I was feeling like I had just finished drinking a cup of nectar from a golden goblet, only to find a dead bug at the bottom.

He kept quiet for an unbearably long period of time.

If I were to bet money on it, he would definitely ask me to wait until February of next year. But Banka was a simpleton. What would he know about leadership opportunities in the financial industry, which are so hard to come by?

'Drop your logic and your vanity.' He said.

Here I was drowning in my brewing conflict and Banka brought on some more pain. I kept my lips sealed.

'I know what your mind is reeling in. You're probably thinking I don't sound logical.' He paused.

'Do you recall what Gurudev once said about how your logic is dependent upon your knowledge and since your knowledge is finite, the logic may not capture all the possibilities . . .'

'And hence it can mislead.' I completed his sentence, invalidating my own feelings. An abysmal feeling of pain was slowly taking over me.

'So are you suggesting that my logic is flawed here? I am keen on relocating. I've landed a really good opportunity that will not wait forever. So why not take a leap of faith?' I meekly protested.

I was being torn apart trying to make sense of it. Everything seemed overwhelmingly difficult.

A month later, in August of that same year, I got up, signed the offer letter that couldn't wait until February, quit my job in New York, packed my bags, and left. I was excited and giddy. Alak didn't share the same excitement for some reason. She was to stay behind and join me later after packing up the apartment in New York. We were confident we'd figure it out somehow. After all, we managed to figure everything out thousands of miles away from home when we first came to the US. And now we were moving back home, back to our comfort zone. How could anything go wrong?

I kept reassuring myself, but somewhere inside, something felt wrong.

It felt as if I had ignored the turbulence warning from the control tower just because all the dials in the cockpit appeared to be perfect and suggested otherwise in that moment.

The Sign

The wound is the place where the light enters you.

—Rumi

After returning, I lay down roots in Mumbai—a city surrounded by such a heightened state of entropy that the frenzy of New York doesn't even come close. It is a city of struggles. There is a struggle for everything from finding work to getting to work. It is a city of extremes, where close to half of its residents live in slums, while it also harbours one of the world's largest concentration of billionaires.

Despite all the challenges of settling in there, I somehow had this growing sense of acceptance towards everything and everybody. The usual me would have lost it by now, but I was managing surprisingly well. Some days, I was able to handle issues so gracefully that even I was surprised. That said, I would still have my days.

However, like unwanted thoughts sneaking their way into a calm mind, soon the imperfections of the city started to become evident as the shine faded with the passage of time.

It had nearly been four weeks. I was living out of a hotel. My evenings were spent searching for an apartment, a place that I could call home. I couldn't find anything that was nice, affordable, and close to work. They say that in a city like Mumbai, only two of the three were possible at any given time.

'Not now. After February.' Every once in a while, Gurudev's words would ring in my ears, and suddenly my restless mind would feel even more anxious.

One evening, I was on my way back from yet another unsuccessful open house. I was tired after a long day of work. Moreover, I was frustrated with the long, drawn-out house-hunting process. The unforgiving Mumbai monsoon was in full swing, and the rain was coming down heavily. I was now hungry, dejected, and had been waiting nearly fifteen minutes for a taxi in the pouring rain. I sheltered under an umbrella that was beginning to look like the skeleton of a battered Dilophosaurus.

In a sea of people, I felt alone. There was no Banka, no Alak, and my family was an overnight train ride away.

In that moment, I regretted the decision to move back to India. Andy Bernard of *The Office* had once said that he wished there was a way to know you're in the good old days before you've actually left them. I could definitely relate.

With no other options left to exercise, I closed my eyes and prayed to the universe to take it easy on me.

Just then an old black and yellow Fiat taxi rushed past, splashing so much water from a puddle along the way that I was drenched from head to toe.

'Son of a . . .' I cried in exasperation. Clearly, the universe was not listening.

The taxi stopped and the driver signalled for me to jump in. I sat in the taxi and slammed the ill-fitting, rusty door. As soon as I could close the umbrella inside the dimly lit cab, my eyes landed on a picture of Gurudev on the taxi's dashboard. He had a serene smile on his face behind the long locks of hair. He was perhaps smiling at how a little adverse situation had completely thrown me off balance. The taxi driver kept asking me where I wanted to go.

'Do you know him?' is all I could ask when my ability to talk eventually returned.

Perhaps it was a sign from the universe. I don't know why, but I felt as if I was not alone.

I vaguely remember telling the driver the address. My eyes involuntarily closed again. I found myself resting in a deep ocean of silence. There were cars honking, people talking on the outside, and unstoppable rain making its way through the permanent gap in the windowpane, but I rested in silence, unperturbed by the world around me. I had lost track of time. My eyes opened when I faintly heard the driver announce that we had arrived.

That evening, on the ride back to the hotel, something inside me had changed for good. My complaining mind had stopped abruptly in its tracks. My awareness had shifted as the feeling of calm took over. My mind had snapped out of its negativity.

I wanted to go see him. I don't know why, but I wanted to be in his presence.

I booked my tickets for Bangalore.

The Ashram Life

Like a tired traveller who yearns to get home, where would you go when the journey of life wears you down?

The traffic finally started thinning out and green patches became more and more visible as we drove southwards from the city of Bangalore. The rapid pace of urbanization hadn't spared this remote part of the sprawling city. Construction for a new elevated metro train line and the resultant widening of roads had created detours and traffic jams in the most unexpected places.

I tried to reach Banka. I was sure he'd be happy to know that I was going to the ashram to meet with Gurudev. The taxi driver's love of talking, though exhausting, kept me from having a conversation with Banka for the nearly two-hour journey from the airport to the Art of Living ashram. I was both astonished and a little terrified, at how he could drive while constantly looking at me in the rear-view mirror—as if his lack of eye contact with me was somehow insulting.

I was keen on seeing Gurudev. However, the closer I got to the destination, the more anxious I grew. Perhaps, a disappointing experience from the past was stirring up some unpleasant memories. And maybe that was also the reason why I had kept postponing this trip.

Back in the late nineties, I had hitchhiked my way to Osho's Ashram in Pune, India. By then, I had heard and read so much about him that I just couldn't resist the urge to check it out. So, I went.

Living on a student's budget, I had managed to make it to Pune after a series of unpleasant events, including a sixteen-hour unreserved train journey from my home. Tired and broke, I was so excited to finally be at the entrance of Osho's Ashram, but I could go no further than that. The person at the gate asked me to take a mandatory HIV test. Quickly deducing that the ashram's prerequisite did not align with my idea of meditation, I turned away disappointed. I questioned whether this path agreed with the quest I had constructed in my mind. And that was that.

Now here I was, over a decade later in Bangalore, making another attempt to get past the entrance of another ashram. The unassuming entrance by a bend in the road would have been easy to miss, if not for a life size image of Gurudev on a large billboard.

We had arrived. Immediately, a security guard made his way over to the car. After giving me a big smile and basic directions, he let us in. No HIV tests or other crazy prerequisites. I was already feeling better.

The ashram distinctly set itself apart from the surrounding land. The space was lush and green. Mature trees provided much-needed cover from the sweltering sun. People generally seemed happy and helpful. This was my first visual impression. My mind had settled. It felt as if I had been transported to a very different era.

I found the room where I would be staying for the next few days. It wasn't anything fancy, but it was squeaky clean. The wooden accents gave it a rustic appearance. I relaxed and waited for my guide. As I looked out the window at the calm surroundings, I began to wonder what the coming days would be like. I tried my best to resist romanticizing what they would entail, as I imagined meditating under a shaded tree in a perfect Buddha posture.

A knock at the door reminded me that enlightenment would have to wait. 'Jai Gurudev, I'm Govind!' A well-mannered young man in his late twenties greeted me enthusiastically as I opened the door. We set out to explore the ashram.

As we sauntered through the grounds, I appreciated that the ashram today looked nothing like what it did when it was first established. I had seen some images of the ashram from the time of its humble beginnings. There was hardly any vegetation or grass. The rocky, barren terrain with reddish-brown soil was all one could see back then. The transformation was incredible—almost unimaginable.

Gurudev's sister, Bhanu, has published a biography of Gurudev that chronicles how he had chosen the physical location for the ashram in the early eighties. She vividly recalls how they squeezed themselves into their father's white Ambassador car and drove south. Just as they reached the current location of the ashram, Gurudev asked his father to stop the car. 'To our right, we could see some hillocks—bare and reddish in hue,' she writes. Gurudev got down and started walking towards the five hillocks. He took a few steps and said, 'This is it.' And the rest, they say, is history.

I imagined a time lapse of the ashram grounds over the last thirty-something years. How the blades of grass would have cut through the red soil and small saplings would have evolved into dainty plants that were now tall and inviting trees.

The ashram was dotted with several meditation spaces. The biggest one, where most of the action seemed to happen, was a modern tubular structure with an arched roof—as big as a massive hangar that could house a couple of Boeing aircraft. No walls and sky lights made it appear spacious and well lit.

Just then, a loud thud made me jolt—it was as if a brick had fallen on the metal roof. Govind matter-of-factly acknowledged the presence of monkeys. Slowly, a bunch of them began launching themselves onto the roof one by one after swinging from a tall tree nearby. It reminded me of Gloria, a friend of mine from New York, who had come to attend a silence retreat here. One fine morning, Gloria was meditating in one of the gardens. When she opened her eyes, she saw a monkey sitting in front of her, chomping on something with his eyes closed. He opened his eyes too. As their eyes met, Gloria let out a shriek that was heard throughout the ashram. The monkey, however, did not take it personally and simply walked away.

Govind laughed like a child as I narrated this incident to him.

Govind led me on a winding trek to the oldest part of the ashram. As we walked under the thick canopy of trees, he proudly shared how the ashram was home to many birds, insects, and plant species. Based on the ease with which he was quoting these statistics, I imagined he must be very comfortable with numbers.

'Do you have a math background Govind?' I casually asked out of curiosity.

He laughed as if I had said something ridiculous. He then ironically told me that his background was in drugs and alcohol. As we continued our walk, he shared how he ended up here.

Once Gurudev had visited Govind's village and was appalled to see that the youth had succumbed to drugs and alcohol. He immediately called all the youth of the village to the ashram and promised them that Sudarshan Kriya would give them a better reward. It wasn't easy. Young people like Govind were addicted to free money doled out by unscrupulous politicians. Gurudev designed a training program for these youths. Govind recalled how initially, they would all come just for the free food. But slowly, after just a few days of the program, they started noticing a difference. The cobwebs that surrounded their consciousness thinned out. Everyone who finished the program went on to do something meaningful with their lives.

Govind, a graduate of the first Youth Leadership Training Program, went on to become a trainer for the same program, giving meaning to the lives of thousands of capable youth just like him.

Later, at dinner, I met several international groups, including a large group of volunteers from South America, the Middle East, and one from China. Govind told me what an amazing job the groups from Brazil and Argentina did at the ashram.

'Except when Brazil is playing Argentina in a soccer match of course. That is when all bets are off!' he qualified.

As I looked around, I realized that I had never met so many people from all walks of life in one single day. They all looked so free and content, with not a worry on anyone's face. They were all from different corners of the world, enjoying the same simple and clean meal. Different skin colours, different religions, different socioeconomic backgrounds, and entirely different traditions. The only thing they had in common was Gurudev and his knowledge.

Once, in Germany, Gurudev had tossed me a bag of nutty trail mix and asked me if I knew what it was.

'It is Art of Living in a nutshell. A bag of assorted nuts!' he said. The entire room burst out laughing.

'Art of Living is a very heterogeneous organization. It is a zoo!' Gurudev jokes often. The ashram appeared to be a microcosm of that idea.

Never before in my life had I imagined myself enjoying an ashram. Our surroundings impact our energy. Sometimes the place itself has an uplifting atmosphere. Perhaps it was because thousands of people had meditated in this place. As I lay my head on the pillow that night, I thought of the Burning Man festival. So many common philosophical traits are found there—inclusion, self-reliance, communal effort, and civic responsibility . . . the list goes on. However, it comes to life only once a year for a few days, in a temporarily erected city. The ashram, on the other hand, was evidence that there is a place where these human values are a permanent way of life.

Walk like a King

Being there for others is the most self-serving act. For uplifting others uplifts you.

The next day, I continued exploring the ashram on my own. After spending just one day in this space, I was already feeling relaxed. Noting had really changed in my personal circumstances, yet my mind was so much more at ease.

As I took a leisurely walk by the lake and the landscaped gardens, I was drawn to the faint sound of ancient Sanskrit chants. It felt very soothing. The sound grew louder as I walked past the gardens in its direction. As I turned the corner, my eyes rested upon a group of boys who were around the age of ten. Bare chested and clad in white wraparounds, chanting in perfect harmony. Sitting in a gazebo covered by a thatched roof, the boys' hands rose and fell in unison with the cadence of the chants. At the far end of the gazebo stood a Ganesha idol. Ganesha, the elephant-headed God known to bestow wisdom, make new beginnings, and remove obstacles. I mentally bowed down to Ganesha, for I could use some serious help in each of those areas.

Several oil lamps hung from the wooden rafters. A mild fragrance of sandalwood lingered. The vibrations from this group chanting were palpable in the air. It felt like I had been transported to a Vedic school from thousands of years ago. I sat there for some time, soaking it all in. I was awestruck and happy to see these students studying a tradition that is no longer prevalent.

Just then, I notice a crowd moving towards me in a familiar way. I hoped it was Gurudev. Everyone was trying to keep up with the man leading the group. Gurudev recognized me and waved. He was wearing sunglasses, so from a distance it was hard to tell if he was actually waving at me. I stood there motionless.

'When did you come?' He stopped and asked.

'Just yesterday, Gurudev.' I kept my response brief.

'This is your first time here, isn't it? Are you comfortable?' I was touched by his simple gesture.

I responded affirmatively. I wanted to talk to him, but the crowd made it difficult to continue the conversation. He signalled that he would see me later. I joined the crowd and followed him up the hill on an unpaved, winding path.

A few years later, Gurudev would share stories of the early days of the ashram. Some of my most cherished times are when Gurudev shared stories with me.

He told us that once, while standing on the top of the barren hill, a vision of the future had flashed through his mind. He saw hundreds of thousands of people visiting the ashram. He could see where the kitchen would be. The kitchen that feeds millions every year today did not exist back then, and the location Gurudev was pointing at had not even been a part of the ashram. At that time, there were barely a hundred people with him, yet he was talking about hundreds of thousands.

'The whole idea appeared to be so far-fetched from reality that people around me thought that I had lost it,' Gurudev said.

He also spoke about the blueprint of the ashram as he envisioned it.

'I wanted to develop our ashram bearing an ancient rustic look; the way it would have been some 5,000 years or so ago,' he said. He could hear other people whispering to each other that it was too impractical and far-fetched. Gurudev recalled smilingly, 'I went ahead with my utopian plans anyway.'

The slopes were left rocky and barren, with somewhat undefined pathways carved through them. The various structures were made with natural materials; cottages were constructed using stones and mud, and rooftops were covered with bamboo mats, coconut leaves and rice straw. However, these basic structures could not even protect against the rain. Natural materials allowed scorpions and snakes to easily sneak through. I imagined the orchestra of insects either feasting on or otherwise disturbing the sincere meditators.

'Eventually, we had to let go of my fantasy to build a rustic-looking ashram, incorporating more conventional methods and compromising on the overall design elements.'

My mind was perplexed when I heard Gurudev say that. At times, he could see how thousands would come to the ashram, but at other times he couldn't tell that a rustic ashram would not hold up against the forces of nature.

Before I made it to the top of the hill behind the crowd, I was intercepted by a young man dressed in white, who was walking in the opposite direction. 'Gurudev is asking you to help out with the distribution of clothes.' The ashram volunteer summoned me.

To celebrate the completion of a Homa—a vedic fire ceremony—the ashram was donating clothes to the needy in the nearby villages. I was instructed to go to Radha-Kunj, a leafy garden by the lake on the other side of the ashram, where the poor villagers had gathered. In my mind I imagined it to be a quick errand, upon completion of which, I could return to Gurudev.

Three of us were to distribute clothes to a line of men. A few others were taking care of a similar line of women. The volunteers brought in a sack full of new garments. My job was to take out a shirt and hand it to the person in line and move on to the next one.

Growing up in India, I had seen a lot of poverty, but a decade of living in the US had taken me away from the harsh reality. Today I was thrown into the fire again.

I slowly began giving away clothes. Their hands extended out. Shaking. Palms open. Their palms appeared hard and dry with callouses. The kinds one develops with strenuous labour. Their eyes had so much innocence and purity.

'Bhaiya, O' Bhaiya. (Brother, O' Brother). Please. Here.' They plead earnestly, ensuring I didn't inadvertently miss any of them as I walked past.

The volunteer would keep bringing in more sacks of garments. I would keep handing them out. The gratitude on the face of the people was unmistakable. They laughed with joy. I was overcome by a bittersweet feeling. I had hardly done any physical work, but I felt completely drained by the time I reached the end of the line. The pleas for help rang in my head even after I was done. My heart ached as if someone had driven a dagger through it.

At some level, there was no difference between any of them and me. Yet, our lives had played out so differently. Why? I sat motionless by the lake after I was done.

Later that evening, I got an opportunity to meet Gurudev. Until that afternoon, I had fully rehearsed what I wanted to share with him about the trials and tribulations of my life in Mumbai. I wanted to ask him if he thought I was on the right track. I don't know why, but somewhere I wanted him to tell me things would be okay.

But when I finally met with him, I didn't feel like talking about any of that. It felt trivial. I instead told him how happy and grateful I felt to be at the ashram. And that was that.

I couldn't stop thinking about Govind. He had perhaps been in the same dire situation as many of those villagers. Abject poverty had handed him over to drugs and alcohol. Learning SKY and coming to the ashram had changed his life. Made him confident. And now he was simply paying it forward with whatever little he had. Making a difference, one life at a time. When I asked him what his secret was, he smiled sheepishly.

'Gurudev showed me how to walk like a king and be a perfect servant.' He said, just before giving me one of his signature warm hugs for the day.

When It Rains

The most important spiritual growth doesn't happen when you're meditating or on a yoga mat. It happens in the midst of a conflict. When you're frustrated, angry or scared and you're doing the same old thing, and then you suddenly realize that you have a choice to do it differently . . .

—Anonymous

After the initial struggle of settling down in the old country, I had finally found a firm footing in India. Work was fun and rewarding. The warmth of family felt cosy. I had found my meditating tribe in Mumbai, and I had plugged myself in. Life appeared to have found a sense of normalcy.

And then my world as I knew it started crumbling down in front of my eyes.

It all happened so fast that I could barely understand it, let alone control it. It was as if all the outcomes of unassuming slip-ups had collectively decided to gang up against me.

Alak's health took a nosedive. She developed an acute form of a respiratory tract illness in Mumbai. The doctors couldn't figure out what it was, and the gallons of medicines were doing more damage than the ailment itself. She was forced to leave India and go back to the US to escape the stubborn pathogens. My first mistake—I should not have let her go alone. However, my commitments at work wouldn't let me travel back with her. Besides, we both thought this would be temporary. It wasn't. We persisted with this status quo for nearly eight months. I was trying to make sense of everything while she fought all by herself, halfway across the globe. My personal hailstorm was showing no signs of abating.

Everyone around us and their mothers-in-law had an idea about what we ought to be doing next. We had pretty much closed the door behind us when we left the US. If we went back, we would have to start from scratch yet again. On the other hand, life in India with our family around was so much more rewarding.

The ugly monster of uncertainty stood in front of my eyes, staring at me without blinking. I did not know which way to go. What was the right thing to do? Like a warrior running out of steam, I waited for reinforcements to show up, but they never came.

I even tried to reach Banka. He would share some wisdom and ask me to meditate more often. I cut him off. Another mistake. He kept quiet for the most part. When he spoke, he would advise me to accept the situation and to be strong. 'Pain is inevitable, but suffering is optional.' He would keep reminding me what Gurudev had once said. In that moment, I found his advice to be quite ineffective. Having run out of options, Alak and I decided to leave everything we had built in India and once again relocate to the US. It felt as if we were starting from the beginning, like we did over a decade ago when I had touched down at JFK for the very first time.

I had no job lined up, and the thought of slogging away at yet another company did little to excite me. I wanted to start something on my own. Willingly or unwillingly, I had hit the reset button in life. Looking back, all I had to do was to remain a witness, and my peace of mind would have been protected. But I hadn't been able to live the wisdom in my moment of truth.

It seemed as if life was teaching me the ways of karma. How one's inner tendencies generate their sphere of external circumstances in a subtle way. And how some people get drawn to certain type of experiences in their life.

Being my own boss and controlling my own destiny was a strangely romantic thought at the time. I jumped in headfirst, an act made easy by my 'ready-shoot-aim' attitude to life.

Along with Archi—a fellow meditator and a good friend, I formed a startup venture. Within no time, reality hit us like a sledgehammer—the start-up didn't seem to be going anywhere. It felt as though we had swum halfway across a river. Reaching either bank looked equally difficult, if not impossible. The pain of running a struggling company in uncharted territory was taking a toll on me. I had gone so deep and so fast in so many directions, that I had lost my way back. I had no idea how to turn around. It's like that annoying and unsettling music on your computer that you want to stop, but you can't tell which browser tab its coming from.

Meanwhile, Alak's health was improving, but too slowly. I had once thought that, on my own, I'd be able to control my hours and spend more time looking after her. My grand plans had completely backfired. I found myself working crazy hours, and she ended up becoming the one supporting me. Another error in judgement.

One more misunderstanding cost me a friendship close to my heart. The guilt of that made matters worse in all aspects of my life. I was losing confidence in my own judgement. As a trader, I had a lot of confidence in my ability to make quick and accurate decisions. Apparently, it had failed me when I needed it the most.

I tried so hard to course correct, but things only got worse. By now, the storm was brewing strong. My instinctive reaction was to blame someone. First, I blamed the planets. But that didn't help. I then pointed my gun at Banka. 'You knew what was happening yet did nothing to warn me. You always have some quick comment to make. But radio silence from you when it really mattered.' I was fuming. Banka was silent. My heart sank even further.

Life was swinging like a rudderless ship on a stormy night. While I was steadfastly holding on to SKY and my meditation practice, I was terribly afraid I'd be thrown overboard at any moment.

I couldn't stop regretting the past. Perhaps, none of this would have happened if I had waited until February. I guess I would never find out.

Laughing in Adversity

Is a spiritual path a crutch or a catalyst? Sometimes, it teaches you something. Some other times, it is a life jacket. But at all times, it is an enabler.

What does your support system look like? Is it a crutch or a catalyst?

It had been a year since we had moved back to the US.

My entrepreneurial struggles were showing no signs of slowing down. The previous week had been a period of intense inner turmoil. The sense of balance and security I had come to rely on had all but vanished. My body was fatigued, and my mind was in a complete funk. To take a break from our maddening routine, Alak and I had decided to visit the Art of Living Ashram in Quebec, Canada. I knew that Gurudev was going to be there. I always experienced a peculiar feeling of warmth and unconditional support around him. I could use some of that.

A Canadian autumn always starts with a tinge of melancholy, yet the crispness in the air and the hazy evenings add a unique texture to the surroundings. The autumn foliage in Quebec was at its peak. White birch, pine, and sugar maple trees were showing off their new wardrobe, and the entire countryside was breathtaking. But when the mind is not at ease, nothing gives joy.

Nestled amidst this setting, in the heart of one of the most beautiful forest regions of Mauricie National Park, rests the quaint Art of Living Ashram, sprawled across acres of natural surroundings.

Close to the main entrance of the ashram stands an unassuming, three-storey wooden building, which hosts one of the first meditation halls built within the ashram. Before it was constructed, the workshops were carried out in tents. I could almost envision it—a small group of smiling, long-haired meditators strumming guitars and refusing to wear deodorant.

That evening, the meditation hall was packed. Some people even sat on the large windowsills overlooking a picturesque lake. Many others were standing in the back. The sun was setting on the distant horizon. A gentle breeze from the westerly window made the candles in the room flicker. One could feel an intense but delicate presence in the room.

Gurudev was at the front of the room, sitting on a small couch, deep in meditation. The lights in the room were subdued. I was sitting on the floor in a corner, and my view of him was partially blocked by a slender, white column. The soothing chants of kirtans filled the room, creating waves of uplifting energy. I keenly observed everyone. People in the room seemed to be happy and peaceful at the same time. This put me even more on edge. I badly wanted that feeling, but given my current mindset, it seemed out of reach.

The singing concluded, and Gurudev opened his eyes after a long meditation.

'Hmmmm?!' The familiar conjecture appeared again. 'Are you all happy?' He asked right out of the gate. The crowd responded affirmatively in a loud chorus.

'Nooo!!!!' I screamed in my head. 'I am miserable. Help!'

I felt even more isolated.

'Pierre, do we have any questions in the basket?' he asked the person sitting next to his couch, who had been collecting questions from the audience. Although Pierre's flowing white beard covered most of his face, his pleasant smile shone through.

'Dear Guruji, how should I deal with a failure?' Pierre read as soon as he uncurled a piece of paper from the question basket.

My ears perked up. Clearly, I was not the only ugly duckling in the barnyard. Somebody else was hurting just like me. I scanned the room in the hope that I could somehow identify this other misfit. Misery loves company after all.

'Do you want to hear a Mullah Nasruddin story? I think I've already told this story before,' Gurudev asked.

A slight smile crossed my face. Mullah Nasruddin is an ancient Persian folk character whose tales have been used for teaching lessons, especially in South Asia. In the past, I have heard Gurudev explain esoteric concepts using Mullah's parables. I wondered what he had up his sleeve that day.

In his inimitable style, Gurudev began narrating the story of Mullah, who once got into a very bad accident. The poor guy had multiple fractures all over his body, and pretty much every part of his face was bandaged. A friend of his came to visit Mullah in the hospital, where he lay in pain.

'How are you Mullah?' the visitor asked.

'Oh, I'm fine. It only hurts when I laugh,' Gurudev asserted Mullah's response with a smile on his face.

The perplexed visitor began to think that Mullah had completely lost it.

'What is there to laugh, Mullah? Have you looked at yourself? How could you laugh in this condition?' asked the concerned friend.

Gurudev paused. One could have heard a pin drop on the carpeted floor.

'If I don't laugh now, I have never laughed in my life,' said Mullah.

More silence in the room.

'Everyone can laugh when things are going well. It takes tremendous courage to smile through when the world around you comes crumbling down,' Gurudev said with a level of conviction I had never seen before.

He continued to elaborate on the topic, but I zoned out. I couldn't help but feel as though he was talking just to me. I needed to hear this. And I had to drive eight hours from New York to do that. It made complete sense, but how could I achieve that enlightened state of mind?

Gurudev ripped open this topic, talking about how the disappointment of failure is amplified by underlying desires.

'Just before a desire arose in you and after a desire completes, where are you? Have you noticed?' He asked the everyone in the room. By the look of his face, I could tell it was definitely a trick question.

'The same place.' He quipped. The answer had now created more questions in my mind.

How? I had really never thought about that. He continued. 'And in the process of fulfilling the desire, one loses the sight of the self.'

'You don't lose the self . . . you just lose the sight of it, hence the restlessness and agony,' he added.

My mind was always on the run. Desires arose. I started chasing them. In that chase I was sometimes happy, sometimes miserable. Most of the time, my desires were fulfilled. When that happened, it boosted my ego and brought some satisfaction. Then I went back to the same place that I was in before that desire had arisen in the first place. And repeat. I was beginning to appreciate the big picture that had just been revealed.

Was there any point in chasing desires? Did I really have a choice to not chase them?

'It is like being on a merry-go-round. You start and get off at the exact same place, having gone nowhere.'

As the evening concluded, the waves of negativity in me had somewhat subsided. I wondered what had changed. The problem at hand remained the same. So did my circumstances. However, in that moment, I could detach from the thick wave of negativity that had enveloped me. I could see how easily I had lost sight of the self, the inner space that is always joyful and at peace.

Like the flip of a switch, Gurudev had helped flick my awareness from the scenery to the self.

You Continue

It is not down on any map; true places never are.

—Herman Melville

How would a lost hitchhiker feel if a completely unknown force were to deliver him to his destination? Ask me.

An entrepreneur's journey is like a never-ending game of darts. From morning till night, one keeps throwing darts at the wall, hoping that one of them sticks. Having found that nothing has stuck, and what has stuck is way off the mark, one starts again. Archi and I were becoming really proficient at this. Stumbling, failing and learning—on repeat. I had been reduced to a dart-throwing machine that operated nearly seven days a week. Despite feeling physically and emotionally drained, I kept pushing my body and spirit. Every time I felt I couldn't take it anymore,

I would plateau out at a new low. Then I would push again, but then boom—another low.

Our stress levels had become inversely related to our bank balances, which were in uncontrolled free-fall. I was on the verge of calling it a day, joining the long list of failed start-ups. Again. I was hanging on by a thin thread of SKY and meditation.

That summer, Gurudev was travelling around the US and visited New Jersey for a public talk. Alak and I had driven down to see him. I was desperate to speak to him. All this time, I had observed numerous people come to him with their problems, small or existential, and pour their hearts out. Gurudev always listened and guided like a genuinely caring friend. Besides, I was out of options. I was desperate for a sign. And I needed him to tell me that it was okay to fail. That it wasn't a big deal after all. Or something to that effect. I don't know why, but it was important for me to hear that from him. Banka was very emphatic about how I should share everything that was going on and get Gurudev's feedback. He had been telling me this for quite some time now. Like a persistent fly, I continued to swat his advice away. But now I was fraught.

After the public talk, I somehow made it to the place where he was staying. It turned out that I was not the only person who had chased him down. Many were eager to see him. I patiently waited for my turn. He saw me and welcomed me with a smile. We exchanged pleasantries and he asked me how I was. I couldn't open my mouth. My mind had gone from sixty to zero in two seconds. In a familiar dynamic, the turbulence in my head had once again disappeared. I had rehearsed my succinct pitch in my mind, but the words wouldn't come out. As I was about to leave, he gave me a piece of fruit. Then through his gestures and his eyes, he asked me what was really going on.

'Gurudev, I can't take it anymore. This start-up is getting very painful, and it seems we should shut it down. Should I just do it?' I was looking for sympathy and words of comfort that would help nurse my deep wounds. He closed his eyes for a couple of seconds. He opened them and looked into mine.

'No. Not now. You continue.' He said, as if he knew what lay ahead.

What? By the time I could even grasp his response, the person eagerly waiting behind me had almost thrown his newborn into Gurudev's arms. Once again, I received a response that I was not prepared to hear. I wasn't going to give up this time around though. I wanted to make sure Gurudev understood the context, and that I heard the answer right.

'So Gurudev, are you suggesting I don't shut it down?' I asked again.

He just gave me a thumbs up.

That day, I drove home in disbelief. The outcome of the meeting had not been what I had expected. Just like the time when I had asked if I should consider relocating to India. And how could he tell me to continue without even knowing the complete picture? It felt like déjà vu.

I felt like a tired soldier in a losing battle whose battalion chief had just commanded him to go all out in a last-ditch effort.

Anyway, we had one last month's worth of savings in the bank. After that, we wouldn't be able to pay the vendors and the curtains would be drawn automatically.

So, Archi and I decided to keep at it.

On Faith

Life is a mystery to be lived, not to be solved.

—Gurudev

Faith is perhaps one of the most misunderstood of all the words. At some point in life, I considered it to be the last refuge of the weak. I could never leave anything to chance. I preferred everything figured out. Proven and scientifically validated.

Let's put things in perspective. Somewhere out there, in a remote corner of the observable universe, lies one of the two trillion galaxies. Travelling at the speed of light—approximately 670 million miles per hour—it would take 1,00,000 years to cross this galaxy, also known as the Milky Way. And during this voyage, there is a very small probability that, along the way, one may run into an insignificantly small blue-green planet, whose seven billion inhabitants know little about what lies beyond their world. You and I are one of them. And on this little planet, each one of us has created the little bubble of our own world. I was at the centre of my personal bubble of life. Within that, I fought with the circumstances until I could solve them. Sometimes it worked. Many times it didn't. When it didn't work as per my expectations, I felt frustrated and helpless. And every time that happened, the universe gently tapped me on my shoulder, reminding me again and again that there is a much bigger power out there that is intelligent, loving and ready to help. The only caveat, I have to be accepting and willing.

The first such instance that I can clearly remember took place in Germany. That day, I was to fly with Gurudev from Frankfurt to New York. In the morning, at the ashram in Bad Antogast, Germany, Gurudev asked me to leave for the airport an hour earlier than planned. I wondered why. Eventually, traffic did slow us down a lot, but the real problem unfolded at the check-in counter when the lady told me that she couldn't find my reservation in the system. What? A copy of the confirmation email from my travel agent didn't help matters. Against the annoying clicking sound of her long nails on those white-turned-beige keyboard, I stood there listlessly staring at her expressionless face. Nearly an hour and a half passed in a drama featuring the attendant, her manager, a ticketing agent, and me. Realizing there was nothing more I could do, I finally relented. I stepped out of the way and let the universe do whatever it wanted.

Alak and I had the biggest fortune to host Gurudev at our home when he had come to inaugurate the first International Day of Yoga in New York at the United Nations in 2015. On this momentous occasion, I managed to ruin his wardrobe. The day he arrived, he handed me a bag full of clothes to take care of. I'm always happy whenever he gives me any responsibility, no matter how small. He had been on the road for over a month already and was on his way to South America, so he had pretty much emptied his entire suitcase.

As I was running around, I delegated the responsibility to a dear friend who felt equally thankful to do it. Unfortunately, she used the wrong setting on the dryer, causing the colours to bleed. My face turned pale when I saw that every one of Gurudev's traditional white kaftans and wraparounds had turned bright pink and patchy. The dignified white garments had turned into bright, flower-power, hippie outfits.

Luckily, by then, Gurudev had left early to lead yoga and meditation in Times Square. A few of us stayed back, including Alak and Banka. We tried every cleaning solution and bleach in town to get the pink off the delicate cotton. It didn't help. We washed them again and again and again, but nothing changed. We tried to replace them with new ones. That didn't work either. In an act of desperation, we even chanted to the clothes. They didn't listen. The clock was ticking. I, unfortunately, had to go make final arrangements for the next evening's plans. We finally stood in the balcony holding the ends until the clothes were dry. Solemnly, we put the garments with kaleidoscopic prints on hangers and neatly placed them in the closet. I was furious, frustrated and disappointed with myself.

This would definitely go on my resume. There were no more clothes left for the rest of the South American tour. I was sure to be reprimanded by Gurudev for sabotaging his wardrobe in the middle of the tour. I apologized to Gurudev in my mind. Defeated, I bowed out silently as I drove home.

Letting go or accepting is not the same as dropping something. When you drop something, you have decided to stop pursuing the matter. On the other hand, letting go simply means making way for a greater power to take over. Having faith.

Faith begins with acceptance—an empowering response to a tough situation, which has not yet changed. A sense of comfort that somehow the dots will connect precisely as they are meant to be.

As I moved away from Lufthansa's check-in desk, I heard a ding followed by some furious typing on the white-turned-beige keyboard. 'Sir, your name just popped up in the system.' The lady announced with a totally confused expression on her face. Before I could make sense of it, she handed me my boarding pass. After reaching New York on that flight, I attempted to narrate my ordeal to Gurudev. He just smiled and winked.

The professional training of Wall Street never made it easy for me to work on faith. One is used to dotting every *i* and crossing every *t* in an eager effort that leaves nothing to chance. I imagined my boss' face if I told him to take it easy and let the universe take care of a deal.

That day when I reached home, I had no idea what I would do about the stained clothing. As soon as I stepped out of the elevator, Shubhra came running towards me in the hallway. She screamed my name in a state of utter disbelief, her eyes ready to pop out. 'The clothes have turned white!' she exclaimed as she hugged me. Even today, none of us know what really happened behind the closet doors.

Faith transcends logic. But once you experience the magic it brings in life, perhaps there is no further empowering feeling.

Gurudev's instruction 'to continue' running our start-up, even when every part of me was begging to shut it down, perhaps meant, 'Now that you have done all you could, just get yourself out of the way and give the universe a chance to perform.' Less than a month after taking that leap of faith, in a sequence of rapid and unexplainable events, we received a buyout offer out of nowhere. According to the yardstick that the world uses to measure success, it had landed. We became a success story overnight.

Like a caring teacher who repeats the same concept several times to a slow student, the universe remained persistent and patient with me while I took time to understand what faith really is. It is all about stepping aside and giving permission to the universe to flip the difficult situation into a miracle. On the other hand, logic demands to only trust that which you know. But where is the fun in that?

When He Asked and I Said . . .

The mind has a tendency to postpone good work. It wants to wait for that perfect moment to commit that perfect action. There is never a perfect time. And no action is perfect either. The only thing that can be perfect is the intention.

—Gurudev

The other day, on a long flight from New York to Los Angeles, I was reflecting on how much I had progressed since that Guru Purnima in Chicago a few years ago. I like to do two things on an airplane—listen to Chopin, especially when the plane is taking off, and introspect when it's high in the sky. Both work very well with the mood and the motion.

Guru Purnima. In the Vedic tradition, it is one of the full moons of the year that is dedicated to the master. It's a little like Mother's Day, but for seekers. For the last few years, Alak and I had made it a point to go see Gurudev wherever he was on that day. It was just our little way of saying thank you for everything. Not that he ever expected that. It was also an excuse to be with him.

A few such moons ago, somewhere in Chicago, Alak and I ended up in Gurudev's room after the day's festivities.

The Guru Purnima celebrations usually start with Gurudev performing an ancient ceremony for the lineage of masters, thanking them for having passed down their wisdom from generation to generation like a prized trophy. A few thousand people join him in the audience. By the time he is done, the entire hall becomes so meditative that it is difficult to keep your eyes open. Gurudev leads everyone into a deep meditation, after which an unmistakably high-energy session of singing follows. I meditate until I am trampled by folks dancing and bouncing off the walls. After that, I too can't help myself and join them, disrupting more and more meditators. The chain reaction continues until almost every person is on their feet. And then comes the best part. Gurudev walks around and meets every single person in the room. Sometimes it takes him hours. And the crowd of people waiting to meet him doesn't deter him.

That day, the room was filled with gratitude. Everyone seemed insanely happy and firmly established in the present moment. It was a space where I couldn't care less about spiritual growth or enlightenment. I could just be in the presence of that soft, fluffy energy.

Gurudev was about to retire for the day after the busy evening. Alak and I were strategically hanging out on his floor. As Gurudev walked into his room, he gestured for us to follow him. Like two kids at a carnival, we followed him into the room, only to find that there were at least fifty other people inside. We stood silently in a corner. I was just happy to be there. I wondered why all these people couldn't leave him alone. They had already met him earlier that day. I communicated my sentiments to Alak with my eyes. 'How were we any different in that regard?' She responded in the same language. Point taken.

Just then, Gurudev called us closer. He asked us if we were happy. His face had a different type of glow. His forehead was beaming. I first thought there must be a halogen lamp reflecting off him. But there was no such light source around.

My grandmother, Hira, used to make an analogy that didn't make much sense back then, though it would tickle my imagination. She would say that nature gave everyone an invisible cup. As a child, I always imagined a cup with Mickey Mouse on it.

'When you meditate, your cup gets filled with the feeling of abundance.'

'And when you do Seva, which means help others without wanting anything in return, you can empty your cup.' She would say this, fully aware of what I'd ask next.

'Why don't you just keep it filled?' I would walk straight into it.

'Because my dear, when you empty it fully, nature gives you an even bigger cup!' She would say. And then she would tell me all the stories about my great grandfather, who had dedicated his entire life to the welfare of his community.

'Gurudev, how could I serve more?' I asked him. Alak also echoed the sentiment. I consider myself very fortunate that we are both always in fierce agreement on the big things in life. And if there is a disagreement, one eventually pulls the other in their direction.

He looked at us with a lot of warmth. His eyes were beaming with pride, like that of a father whose children had finally said something sensible. He gently tapped my shoulder and asked us if we'd like to become teachers. I assumed he was asking us to become Art of Living teachers. Alak immediately jumped on it. 'Yes, I would love to Gurudev. I want to go for the teachers training this year.' Gurudev gently acknowledged her with a smile and looked at me.

The other day, I had managed to get my hands on some old tapes of Gurudev's talks. In one of them, he spoke at length about Seva. Even though they have since been digitized, the squeaking of the spools still came through the speakers. The static from the tape was unable to suppress the conviction in the soft voice of Gurudev, who was in his twenties back then. Rarely, some words are so direct and impactful. I listened with my eyes closed as the words filled up the room.

'In your life, each one of you has uttered a few words to somebody at some time or the other. If you need me, I am here.' The voice on the tape paused. 'If these words have not come out from your mouth, then you have been living in fear and distrust.'

Gurudev was looking straight at me. I froze. I didn't know what to say. There was a raging, self-created storm behind the thin veil of my face. I had asked Gurudev how I could be of help. But when he rolled out a perfect platform to make an impact, I couldn't commit to it. Not because I doubted the platform. But because I felt that becoming a teacher would be like the biggest act of hypocrisy in my life.

I had debated the idea of becoming an Art of Living teacher with Banka several times before. I always felt that teaching the SKY technique itself was no big deal, but being a teacher meant more than just imparting a set of mechanical instructions. It also involved sharing some of Gurudev's simplest yet most profound principles. One could rely on these basic tenets to navigate life's most complex problems and move through them without getting stuck. Therein was the source of my confusion. One of the tenets is about accepting people and situations as they are. If I myself couldn't accept people and situation as they are, how could I give lessons in acceptance? Yet another tenet is about not being tossed around like a football by other people's opinions. And if I couldn't stop myself from being swayed by others' opinions about me, how could I sit on my high horse and ask other people not to be affected by it? I just didn't think it was sincere.

In that moment, a few hilarious stories about some instructors flashed in front of my eyes. There was one fellow who was fascinated by conspiracy theories about the moon landing and the illuminati. This instructor travelled the world teaching meditation but didn't miss an opportunity to discuss his unscientific musings. Then there was another chap who took instructions literally. He must have heard Gurudev talk about how one's vibes speak louder than words. Once he went to a meditation class and just sat there smiling—forcing his vibes to do the talking. In a few minutes, the entire class left, leaving behind the instructor and his vibes. And then there was another one who had been entrusted with introducing meditation to a group of high-society women from London. They all came to hear the wisdom of this Yogi. He started talking about ego and urged the crowd to drop theirs. He asked everyone to kick their shoes off and sit cross-legged on the floor. The women, in their high heels and skirts, were very uncomfortable sitting on the floor. No wonder the organizers never heard from this group again. While all this cracked me up, I couldn't make sense of Gurudev's style. Was it his compassion that let such people continue representing him and the foundation? After all, why would he keep these personalities around him on such a long leash. In that moment, I really questioned how Gurudev could allow such madness to persist around him. And I also asked myself if I really wanted to be a part of this spectacle.

And so, unlike Alak, I kept quiet when Gurudev asked. I just couldn't make myself commit. In my mind, I was thinking, 'It's me. Not you.' He was perhaps having fun reading my juvenile thoughts. I hugged him. He gave both of us some sweets and disappeared into his bedroom.

Six years later, that long flight from New York to Los Angeles was carrying me to one of the most transformational events of my life—the Art of Living teachers training. I was flying high with Chopin in my ears and Gurudev in my heart.

Dancing on the Edge of a Sword

Directions, Debates. Games, Law of Attraction and Spiritual Path. They all exist because of opposites.

One of my biggest hesitations to get on the spiritual path came from the notion that it required me to abandon the fun and exciting aspects of my life. And so, taking up a consistent meditation practice felt as difficult as putting on a saffron robe, shaving my head and going to the Himalayas. Hence, I would always make myself too busy to take up the practice. Refined dispassion had never been my strong suit. Would I eventually lose interest in life if I committed myself to a spiritual path? I was afraid. It appeared only logical to push back such pursuits until after retirement.

After all, what does it really mean to walk the spiritual path?

I often asked myself this question after I got on the path, or should I say after I was thrusted upon it by Banka's relentless efforts. Early on, I would imagine strictly disciplined soldiers marching in profile with their expressionless faces turned in one direction. Sometimes that image would morph into monks watching their breath and meditating all day, forcefully pushing away all sensory pleasures. Neither of these images particularly appealed to me.

I still remember the first Navratri celebrations that I attended at the Bangalore Ashram many years ago. Navratri is to a meditator what Comic-Con is to a comic book and graphic novel enthusiast. In Sanskrit, Navratri literally means 'nine nights,' and it is a time for celebration, meditation, introspection and deep rest.

The ashram hosts a nine-day-long gathering every year. For the past thirty-five years, the celebrations have kept alive the Vedic traditions that go back thousands of years.

Thousands of meditators from all over the world had gathered to take part in the festivities, and the ashram seemed to be bursting at the seams. The volunteers were working around the clock to attend to this sea of humanity. As I walked around the ashram, I could hear conversations in many different languages. There were lines at the gift store, dining hall, juice bar, and even at the restrooms.

With time, my understanding of what it takes to be spiritual changed. The strict and regimented perspective loosened its shackles. A vertical rock climb turned into a moderate hike with many surprises along the way. It had almost become a game. One day, I had an 'A-ha' moment while watching the Super Bowl with some friends back in New York.

Munching on a slice of a pizza, I imagined myself to be the wide receiver in my personal Super Bowl game of life. And my spiritual path was helping me become better and better at gliding through the chase without being knocked over. It was preparing me to be willing and ready to catch whatever life threw at me. Literally.

When I sat for meditations in the beautiful dome-like structure in the ashram, I would almost forget where I was. Then, when I opened my eyes and saw all the people around me, I just wanted to hide in my room. Part of me wanted to leave that place, but another part strongly wanted to stay. There was something in the air. I couldn't quite put my finger on it. Like the unseen yet palpable energy that is experienced when two magnets are brought closer.

On the first day, I didn't go anywhere except the meditation hall and my room. I was staying at the other end of the ashram with roommates from Bulgaria. One of them snored like a freight train at night, forcing upon me an opportunity to practice acceptance. I observed them both and admired how they were so much at home in this faraway land.

By the fifth day, I was moving around the ashram as if I were walking on the streets of New York. I felt completely at home. Despite all of the frenzy around me, my mind was feeling settled and happy. I was also feeling a little confused, unable to understand where this beautiful feeling was coming from. I continued to soak in this apparent contradiction of inner calm and outer buzz.

As I was heading to the dining hall, I spotted some resident volunteers walking about. They appeared rushed but in control. Exhausted but cheerful. A thought crossed my mind. Would I be able to live in the ashram? Would someone like me even fit in? At one level, I felt so complete there. But the very thought of giving up my comfortable lifestyle and work in New York sent chills down my spine.

Various meditations and some singing continued into the evening, followed by a talk from Gurudev, after which he answered some questions.

Two German researchers had come up onto the stage with a laptop. They had a special camera that could capture the aura of living objects using a scientific technique called Kirlian photography. This was the first time I had heard of this.

They presented the pictures they had taken from the mass meditation we did with Gurudev. The entire physical space of the meditation hall, which holds nearly 1,00,000 people, was bathed in a soft yellowish green hue, representing love and healing. They shared how the hue expanded even beyond what the camera could capture. They had never seen anything like this before.

Today, when I look back and connect the dots, I feel that the practice of SKY breathing and daily meditation had created an armour around me. Armour that would also work as a floatation device when I found myself in the deep end. One that would protect me when life jumped on to me like a 300-pound defensive tackle, trying to raze me to the ground and giving me free concussions along the way. If this armour had a colour, it would be a soft hue of yellowish green.

A gentleman from Japan, a successful doctor by profession, grabbed the floating mic in the audience and expressed how difficult it would be for him to eventually go back to the so-called 'real world'. He asked Gurudev, half-jokingly, if he could stay at the ashram forever. I could completely relate to how he felt. I remember being so curious about how Gurudev would field that question. Would Gurudev ask him to leave his world of activity and embrace the simplistic ashram life?

Gurudev smiled at him and responded that doing so would be like staying parked at a gas station. One has to fill up and drive around, and then come back to refill only when the gas tank is empty. Everyone laughed at the analogy. I remember experiencing a strange sense of relief.

Perhaps my biggest concern was the image of meditation as something boring. What was the point of sitting with your eyes closed and observing your thoughts when there was no way to control them anyway! After all, you can't really stop a thought when its time has come.

My mind floated back to Gurudev's response to that gentleman's question. Hidden beneath the humour and simplicity of his response lay the most sought after, yet elusive, of human pursuits.

Life has always felt more meaningful when there is a work-life balance. A country also flourishes only when its economic growth is balanced. Even in the intergalactic world, the Jedi battle was to establish a balance in the Force. The irony is, one only values this balance when things are unbalanced.

'Spirituality is a dance on the edge of a sword between the opposites of life,' Gurudev had once said, while addressing a group at Yale University.

So then, what is it to walk the spiritual path?

With the regular practice of meditation, slowly but surely, it was becoming clear in my mind that I didn't have to make a choice between chasing my aspirations and walking a spiritual path. I could freely pursue both.

The complementary nature of these two aspects felt oddly comforting. It was as if each enhanced the value of the other.

The thought itself was liberating. I could go out and play in the world, enjoy all that the world had to offer. And when I felt drained, I could just go back to my spiritual practices. Back to my gas station. Charge the system and get ready for the world again. Then repeat.

Meditation and enjoying life don't have to be mutually exclusive. Dipping into that inner silence every now and then makes the so-called 'fun part' of life even better. It lends a rich contrast.

In my game of life, I imagined Gurudev as the ultimate quarterback, who knew exactly when and where to pass me the ball so that I could get to the goal without fumbling. But I fumble. He is infinitely patient. He waits for the right time and passes me the ball again. I keep inching towards the goal. Ten yards at a time.

Real Virtual Reality

One needs a matchstick in the dream to light the candle in that dream. The candle of dreams can't be lit with the matchstick from the real world. It is like worrying or fantasizing in the head, which in no way solves anything in the real world. These are two different dimensions. What we think in is a completely different dimension from that we act in.

—Gurudev

I was a little confused, for I didn't know what my reality was. Was it what I could see through these eyes? Was it what I believe in? Dreams don't feel real, but that is only after waking up from them. I called Banka to learn about his reality, but his line was busy.

In one of his most prolific commentaries, Gurudev told the story of a generous and capable emperor, Janaka. A long time ago, his kingdom was one of the most prosperous of the times. One day, Janaka was sitting in his court as his ministers talked about business and read reports. I don't know whether it was monotony or boredom, but he fell asleep in the middle of his court and dreamt that his prosperous kingdom was struck by a horrendous famine. All the glory of the kingdom vanished in this dream. He saw himself as a beggar in tattered clothes, roaming the streets in search of food. But there was no food to be found anywhere.

I once took a virtual field trip to Yosemite National Park, through a virtual reality headset. This little gadget, like a bulged-up Zorro's mask, completely transports you into a different world. When I looked down three hundred feet from the precipice of Vernon falls, my legs began to shake at the mere perception of height. It was surreal—as if I was really there. Even though I knew I wasn't.

And suddenly it occurred to me. How many times has something happened inside my head, which I had believed to be real? Is it like the virtual reality I just experienced? There were moments when I felt lost between what was in my head and what was 'real'. And that reminds me of *Yoga Vasistha*. The handbook of consciousness, as Gurudev calls it.

Reading through it, my eyes rested on a sentence that was written in quite an 'oh-by-the-way' fashion.

This world-appearance is a confusion, even as the blueness of the sky is an optical illusion. Neither freedom from sorrow nor realization of one's real nature is possible as long as the conviction does not arise in one that the world-appearance is unreal.

—Yoga Vasistha

While roaming the streets of his once prosperous kingdom in search of something to eat, Janaka's eyes fell upon a piece of dry bread. He picked it up. And just when he was about to eat, an eagle swooped in, snatched it from his hand, and flew away. He suddenly woke up from this dream and found himself back in his court. He felt a pang of hunger. He was confused. Which one was a dream? The court scene or the famine?

Sitting on the beach in Santa Monica, I watched the waves incessantly lash the shore. If the blueness of sky above me was an optical illusion, was the sand beneath me also an illusion? Could it be that everything I was experiencing at that moment was an illusion? What if I was just in a dream that I had not yet woken up from?

Doesn't a dream state create a surreal feeling of being right there? For months after 9/11, I would dream that I had listened to the security guard's instructions to go back inside the North Tower. Soon the towers would begin to collapse with a deafening rumble, and I'd try to outrun the inevitable. And suddenly I'd wake up sweating, my heart beating fast. It would take a me a few seconds to reconcile the reality of my cosy comforter with the chaos in my dreams. For a few moments, I couldn't decide on my own reality.

Once, Mullah Nasruddin dreamt that he was in the middle of a negotiation, and a man was giving him nine coins, whereas he was demanding ten. Suddenly, in the middle of this, Nasruddin woke up from his sleep. As he looked at his hands, he realized that there were no coins. Being the dedicated businessman he was, he could not leave an open deal on the table. He closed his eyes, opened his hand, and said, 'You win. I'll settle for nine.' But the reality of that dream had already passed.

What portion of what I see and perceive is real? Is this whole world a creation of my own mind? Well, at least that is what the weighty excerpt from *Yoga Vasistha* says. The other day, I was facilitating a SKY Breath Meditation program, and a thought emerged. The future is as elusive as a dream. When I wake up to this present moment, I realize that some forty years of my life have just disappeared. Like a cloud of smoke, there is nothing to hold on to, except for some nostalgia and some unpleasant memories. It all feels like a long dream. I feel like I'm trapped in the Matrix.

An eighth-century Vedic philosopher and a yogi, Adi Shankara, happened to be walking down the street when a crazy elephant started chasing him. Watching the charging elephant, Shankara ran for the shelter.

Shankara was someone who looked at reality as a dream, and he had distilled his thinking in Advaita philosophy. 'This entire manifest world is an illusion,' he would say.

I'm not in agreement with either way just yet. However, I certainly have had experiences in my life where my dream felt real, and my reality felt like a dream.

Looking at Shankara's dash for safety, one of his critics sarcastically asked him, 'Why are you running, Shankara? Isn't the elephant an illusion?'

'If the elephant is an illusion, then so is my running!' responded the smart-witted Shankara.

There's so much depth in this simple response. Einstein's entire space–time construct is hidden somewhere in that answer. When I heard it for the first time, I thought I had grasped it. Turns out, I wasn't even close.

Have you ever wondered about the universe? I've heard theoretical physicists say that our universe may very well be just one in a vast multiverse, potentially comprised of an infinite number of other universes. I want to believe that, not just because I've believed in extra-terrestrial life ever since I watched *E.T.* as a child, but also because thinking that our planet is the only one like it seems to be a statistically insignificant hypothesis. However, I am yet to experience it myself.

Several years later, Gurudev elaborated on how different levels of realities exist in this multiverse. I heard him say. 'What is real in one plane of existence could be an illusion in the other.'

What?!

Suddenly, I was filled with questions about different dimensions and about my very own understanding of the reality that is in front of me.

The current world, my dream state, and the virtual reality experience—if that counts—are all different planes of existence that I have experienced. And I wondered, how many more dimensions were there? What did they look like?

Once, in Canada, a few of us were with Gurudev. The conversation somehow shifted toward the mysteries of the universe. I jumped on this opportunity and asked Gurudev if he had experienced any other planes of existence, beyond the dreaming and waking state.

'There are countless worlds as ours,' he responded casually. For him it seemed to be as obvious as the nose on my face.

He then went on to say that with skill and a broader perspective on life, one can experience the vastness of this creation and obtain the ability to peek into other worlds. I was astounded.

Gurudev continued, 'There is a world out there where nothing is certain. Every moment, everything around you changes into something completely different. You try to sit on a chair and suddenly find that it has turned into a puddle of water. You reach out to drink water and find it has turned into a stone. Unlike the world in which we live in, there is no gradual change in this world. Everything is abrupt. You may be talking to a man, and he suddenly turns into a dog. And in the next moment, that dog turns into a woman. You may be speaking, and suddenly your voice changes. Everything flips within the blink of an eye.' He paused while keeping his gaze on the dark sky outside the window.

What did he just say? I was lost and confused, but at the same time, something told me it was true.

'This extreme state of uncertainty can unnerve you. You might go insane in simply trying to fathom this intense rate of change. You will want to scream out of fright and extreme frustration, but there is nobody to listen to you.'

Just the thought of living in a world like that made me anxious. This could easily fit into the mind-bending universe of *Doctor Strange*.

He continued, 'However, in the middle of this chaos, you find that there is a light within you that remains unaffected. It doesn't change. It guides you. It comforts you and gives you strength to carry on. It helps you calm down. Once you repose in that light, the uncertainty does not impact you anymore. It is the only way to navigate through this world.'

There is always the inner voice, the true north within us that saves the day—but only if we give it permission to do so. Perhaps he was referring to that inner voice.

If I had not been interrupted by an incoming phone call, my dropping jaw would have touched the floor. I was completely stunned—in a mixed state of curiosity, disbelief and awe.

Clearly, there is a lot more out there than meets the eye. At some level, it is like watching television. We immerse ourselves in the channel that we are watching, while other channels broadcast simultaneously. We are quite unaware of what is being shown on these other channels, yet if we flip away from the one that we're watching, the new channel becomes reality while the old one ceases to matter.

I was completely blank in that moment, and as if to stir that blankness, Gurudev brought upon more.

'Stability comes when you log on to something in you that is not changing—that remains the same throughout time.'

A sinking feeling had enveloped the resonance I was experiencing in Gurudev's words. In that moment, all I could do was close my eyes.

King Janaka invited an enlightened master, Ashtavakra, to his palace, confident that he would have the key to the conundrum of what is real and what is not. And then begins one of the most amazing dialogues that has taken place on this planet. Ashtavakra—a man with eight deformities in his physical body—leads Janaka step by step to the knowledge of what reality is.

It was getting dark. I glanced at my watch, nearly an hour had slipped by. A seagull landed within a few feet of where I was sitting, poking his beak into the salty water. I got up to head back to the hotel. As I dusted the fine sand from my clothes, I couldn't help but compare my existence on this planet to a grain of sand in this gigantic multiverse. After all, at one time, that grain of sand had been a massive mountain.

Back to the current reality—my stomach was grumbling, and I wanted tacos.

Eclipse and a Ball of Butter

What if one day you find out that your mind is like a trapeze artist, constantly performing a delicate balancing act on a wobbly tripod?

It was a big night for meditators. It was the night of the last solar eclipse of the decade. Some six planets were in alignment. Gurudev had instructed everyone to eat a light meal and meditate during the eclipse. Apparently, the benefits of meditation multiply manifold during an eclipse.

Gurudev had started talking about a new wisdom series the day before. It was about the trifecta of Desire, Action and Knowledge. Like a person wearing glasses who doesn't realize the presence of a lens between them and the world after a while, these three are so deeply intertwined with our daily lives that we almost lose sight of them. How profound and subtle the play and display of their inner workings is, yet how simple they appear to the unsuspecting.

The talk was held in the main meditation hall of the Art of Living Retreat Centre in Boone, North Carolina. The high energy meditation space—defined by its high ceilings and four curved wooden pillars—had been a silent witness to many such wisdom and meditation sessions. However, this particular series was quite different in flavour.

It had been an eventful few days. It had started with my gate-crashing the first session of the silent retreat. I was not on the retreat, but I still wanted to meditate with Gurudev. Banka would have been so proud. Not. In a fantasy article about the 'Top Ten Crazy Things People Do to Be with Gurudev', my gate-crashing adventure would barely qualify. I got a kick out of it, nonetheless. With a silly smile, I tiptoed my way into the hall while Gurudev was narrating the story about four disciples of a master.

Gurudev was seated on a couch on a stage that was still decorated with Christmas and Hanukkah themes. A nearly six-foot-tall tree adorned the stage, and right next to it was a golden Menorah with six burning candles. Two more to go.

Someone had cracked open the exit door near me. Every now and then a gust of the icy December breeze came through it, only to sting the people obstructing it and then disappear inside the expansive hall without a trace.

I was seated in row eight. Close yet far. Wisdom sessions have a rather predictable effect on me. In a soothing and caring way, they take me to a contemplative and pensive state. And soon after, like a gust of cold air, the wisdom silently vanishes, leaving some breadcrumbs in the form of disjointed thoughts for me to follow home. Hence, that day, I was typing away furiously on my phone as Gurudev spoke.

Each wisdom series has a character. Deep, esoteric, heavy and mystical would summarize a few in the past. This one was light—like a fluffy pancake. And totally relatable. Gurudev was addressing a crowd of nearly 1,000 people. He was helping the crowd observe how the wisdom related to each one of us differently, and then dropping hints on how to implement these teachings.

Heeding to Gurudev's instructions, I retired early and headed to my room just before the eclipse began. Before I sat down to meditate, I unlocked my phone and plunged into the digital equivalent of my shorthand notes. I read them word by word like a linguist poring over an ancient language that no one spoke anymore. One could spend days decoding the possibilities that are hidden in what Gurudev had said earlier that day. Every time I read them, a new understanding dawned. More questions popped up. Desire, Action and Knowledge—three modes of one's consciousness. A desire leads to an action, and knowledge dawns with the completion of that action. There are different types of desires. Some are life supporting, some not so much—but they all lead to action. Action releases the desire. Conscious action liberates—else the cycle continues. The more I thought about this interplay, the more it seemed like a maze with no exits.

I made list of my desires: spend more time with Gurudev, avoid refined sugar, buy a Tesla, grow on the path . . . and someday, have no desires. After all, Buddha said that desire is the root cause of suffering. But isn't not having desires also a desire? Also, how does one not have desires?

His words from earlier in the day came to mind. The root cause of misery had nothing to do with having desires. Instead, it was about hanging on to them.

When you catch and throw a ball of butter, it leaves a thin film on the palm of your hands. It can be wiped away quickly. Desires should be just like that. A thin layer that can be easily done away with. Suddenly, Buddha's words had a new meaning in my mind.

Somebody was talking loudly in the hallway. The voice sounded familiar. Wait, was she VB? I hadn't seen her cross the border and come to the US much.

In the universe of the Art of Living, I have come across two VBs. One is what the seasoned meditators around me have abbreviated the heavy-sounding Sanskrit term

Vigyan Bhairav to. It literally translates to the 'science of consciousness' that Gurudev has elaborated on. Some call it Vigyan Bhairav, others refer to it as 'Unveiling Infinity'. Just like a chocolate affogato, a set of words cannot convey the decadence and layering of hidden flavours—neither name speaks much to me. What it really means to me is a collection of mind-blowing—literally—meditation techniques that were given by a master to a sincere student, also to his other half, who admitted that although she had read everything on meditation and spirituality, all that wisdom felt dry without any tangible experience. It's interesting how thousands of years later, I could deeply relate to her.

The other VB is Vicky Block. A talented artist from Montreal, a long-time meditator, writer, and a self-proclaimed misfit with whom I have at least one thing in common. She too finds it difficult to understand her own spiritual experiences, let alone explain them.

Gurudev had kicked off one of the VB sessions by talking about turning the consciousness inwards with eyes open. If meditating with your eyes closed wasn't tricky enough, now he was talking about doing the same thing with your eyes open. Gurudev suggested that it should be like a skilled driver who can shift gears smoothly without a jolt. I imagined him in the front seat of my rickety old stick shift Fiat. Every time I changed gears, the car would propel itself ahead in a heaving motion that was accompanied by a squirming sound coming from the bowels of the car.

While wisdom sessions like VB are opportunities to let the demystified mysteries of consciousness sweep you off your feet, the evening satsangs with Gurudev sometimes offered something completely different—an opportunity to practice acceptance. At times, someone would ask him a trivial question, or recite subpar poetry written to express gratitude, or ask a long-winded question that already contained the answer. Even after so many years, it amazes me every time how Gurudev deals with this chaos so patiently.

I still vividly remember my first satsang with Alak and Banka. And even after so many years, my buttons get pressed by some of the crazies around Gurudev. These days, when that happens, I often think of Vicky. Either I am entertained by visualizing how she would have somersaulted her way through the funny thoughts in her head, or I am inspired to bolt away from the situation, because that is what I imagine she likely would have done.

Once at a satsang, a lady grabbed the mic and said something completely unexpected in front of thousands of people.

'Gurudev, I want to sleep with you.' She was so earnest in her admission that most of the crowd, including me, felt either shocked, scandalized, or uncomfortable. One could hear nervous scoffs in the room. But before the room could recover from this curveball, Gurudev responded.

'Here I am trying to wake you up, and you talk of sleeping? Come on, wake up!' The crowd erupted in laughter.

All these questioning minds submit like wet noodles when they come remotely close to experiencing infinity during the VB sessions. Even if they had experienced infinity, it would be mathematically inaccurate to say so—it ceases to be infinity the minute it becomes a comprehensible phenomenon.

Gurudev once shared how VB was quite misunderstood. While that sentiment holds true for both of the VBs, he was referring to the scriptures of Vigyan Bhairav. These are a collection of tantra techniques that have been incorrectly portrayed as techniques of sex. Oh Google! You can be so misleading. And that is why it takes a realized master to decode thousands of years old scripture and go beyond what meets the eye.

By the end of the third and last day of VB, I was feeling light as a feather. From resting in the space between in-breath and out-breath to making peace with waiting. From bending the breath like a horseshoe to the mystery of the left toe. All these seemingly unrelated stratagems had only one thing in common. They all gave a glimpse into the seventh layer of existence. The vast, unbounded Self.

When VB and I compared our notes, we had a good laugh at our respective experiences of one of the final techniques in the class—one that required you to balance your entire body on your right butt cheek, with both hands and feet floating in thin air as if in a free fall. That day, I concluded that the only thing more difficult than performing this acrobatic feat was doing it with a thousand pairs of eyes looking and laughing at me. Gurudev had asked me to demonstrate the technique in front of the entire audience. Demonstrating an unfit body in an awkward holding pattern really gave the ego a run for its money.

Gurudev did reveal that the technique could curl the consciousness inwards while keeping the eyes open. Looking back, all that feels like a dream. A dream with my eyes wide open.

The room was silent. The mountains were silent. The wind was blowing through the trees. The trees were silently talking to each other, just like the four disciples of a master. The four of them were sitting on the banks of a river, observing silence and watching the sun set. Just then, a passerby asked them for directions. 'I'm in silence,' said the first disciple. 'You just broke the silence!' said the second one. 'I'm going to complain about you both to the master,' said the third one. 'I'm the only one observing silence here,' said the fourth one. 'Let your silence in the upcoming days not be like theirs!' Gurudev concluded, triggering the silent room to burst into laughter.

My meditation was deep, with little situational awareness afterwards. It must be the effect of the eclipse. The English word 'moon' comes from the Sanskrit word *mana*, which means 'the mind'. Just like the moon was obstructing the light of the sun in the present Solar eclipse, I was wondering how my mana was constantly eclipsing my perception. In meditation, the monkey mind dissolves. A state of doing nothing, wanting nothing and being nothing. When there is no mind, the light of a thousand suns shines bright. Otherwise, I too am a walking eclipse.

The Chaos Theory

It's hard to believe anything without chaos. It's even harder to believe anything else.

—Anonymous

It was a sunny afternoon in St Mathieu du Parc in Quebec. Gurudev happened to be at the Canada ashram.

Fresh snow had further accumulated on mounds that were already six-feet high surrounding the *kutir*, a Sanskrit word which means a spartan accommodation. Just like the aircraft carrying the president of the US assumes the call sign of Air Force One, whichever room or home that Gurudev stays in seems to earn the call sign kutir.

When not out on walks or in meditation halls, Gurudev spends most of his time meeting individuals and teams here. In the main hall of the kutir, volunteers share updates on service projects, teachers share their challenges and celebrate victories and people offload their worries and problems. Gurudev patiently attends to everyone. The door to the kutir leads to a small waiting area that spans approximately 100 square feet. That day, about 100 people were packed into that small waiting room, and another 100 or so were braving the frigid temperatures outside. And every time the door to the kutir opened, the eyes of everyone in the crowd gazed up in anticipation and hope of seeing Gurudev.

My meeting with Gurudev ended, and while I wanted to simply be around him, the meeting room was not big enough for me to stand in a corner and remain unnoticed. With the disappointment of a child who had been asked to switch off his favourite TV show and do his homework, I unwillingly stepped out.

Although practiced, endured or suffered, in various ways and traditions, the unanimous agreement is that nobody likes to wait. People are far from blissful even in the most lavish airport lounges. On the contrary, the group waiting outside Gurudev's kutir was a sight to behold.

As the door opened to let me out, there was a loud cheer, followed by a collective sigh. Clearly, the eager crowds outside were not thrilled to see me at the door.

At one end of the waiting room, a couple of expert photographers were discussing lighter and faster camera lenses that would best capture the master in action. At the other end, a bunch of light-hearted individuals were laughing at silly jokes. A couple of executives with PowerPoint-loaded laptops in their hands were eagerly waiting for their lesson in patience to end, so that they could go meet Gurudev. From the large, almost-French windows, I peeked outside. In the far corner, a group of locals had started initiating interested people into a traditional boot dance—a self-choreographed, catchy routine that gradually increased in tempo and kept everyone warm, while spreading laughter all around. Soon it flew a little out of control, culminating in a snowball fight.

The chaos in the atmosphere was evident, but the familiar sentiment of frustration that usually accompanies such chaos was missing. Gurudev says that waiting is like standing at a fork in the road. One road leads to frustration, and the other to meditation.

A small group of chatty friends were discussing whether it would be prudent to go for a cup of chai. There was fierce disagreement in the group, as some of them didn't want to be left behind if Gurudev came out and met everyone.

Listening to their conversation, a story about a cup of coffee that Gurudev had shared popped into my head.

Imagine you're holding a cup of coffee. Just then, someone comes along and bumps into you, making you spill your coffee all over yourself. Now, what would you say when your friends ask about how you managed to get coffee all over yourself? Your natural response would likely be to simply blame it on the accident. Isn't it? Now here comes the twist. You spilled the coffee because there was coffee in your cup. Had there been chai in the cup, you would have spilled chai.

'When life comes along and shakes you, whatever is inside you will spill out.' Gurudev said. So, what spills over then?

'Joy, gratefulness, peace and humility? Or anger, bitterness, harsh words and reactions?'

The older version of me would have walked away from this fish-market-like atmosphere with a huge frown on my face. But that day, I was able to find the comic relief amidst the chaos.

But would all these people, including me, be so cheerful and accepting if they were not around Gurudev?

Chaos theory is built on underlying randomness. Chaos seldom leads to orderliness, let alone bliss. Like the heads and tails of a coin toss, both of these seem to be mutually exclusive—except around Gurudev. Chaos and bliss appear inseparable. Like the phoenix that rises from the ashes, it is always the former that emerges from the latter. Almost as if by design.

Power of Intention

Intention. Attention. Manifestation. That is how the universe works.

—Gurudev

There was a sea of people on the bank of a river. They all sat facing a mammoth structure that looked like a fully lit starship. But everyone's eyes were closed. There was thick stillness in the atmosphere. A pleasant breeze, like a line drawn on the surface of a still lake, came and disappeared. Led into this sphere of calm by Gurudev, nearly three million souls were meditating in complete silence. I was one of them, accompanied by Alak, Banka and mixed feelings of deep gratitude and even deeper disbelief. All of this started with a simple intention.

Five days ago . . .

The chaos had already begun at the airport. Hundreds and thousands of people were flying in from all over the world to attend the event. I had arrived two days before the festival was to start so I could ease into the Delhi pace. I guess everyone else had the same idea.

While the allure of meditating together with millions drew me in without much hesitation, the excitement of attending a once-in-a-lifetime event seemed to vanish in the pollution-rich air as soon as the rubber tires hit the New Delhi runway. I had absolutely no idea what to expect from this cultural festival—in retrospect, I could have written a memoir on just those three days I spent in India. For someone who wouldn't travel across town to attend a cultural event, flying sixteen hours to get to one was a big deal.

Moreover, I had missed out on Art of Living's twenty-fifth anniversary celebrations ten years ago. Alak and I were not going to miss out on this one. When I asked Banka, he was also very excited.

The day of . . .

We were put up at a hotel just a couple of miles from the venue. A drive that would usually take no more than twenty minutes took a little over two hours on the first day of the event. There were traffic jams on the streets that were further amplified by some 20,000 odd weddings in Delhi that very same day. Impeccable timing.

An average Super Bowl stadium can accommodate 70,000 people. In comparison, this event attracted more than 3.75 billion people—more than fifty times the scale of a Super Bowl game. A production of that magnitude is difficult to imagine, let alone bring to life. A 120-acre venue, sixteen gates, various categories of entry passes, thousands of artists from hundreds of countries, world leaders, politicians and media. There were so many opportunities for things to go wrong in this apparent logistical nightmare.

Just as people settled down, a mild drizzle started unexpectedly. The sun was still above the western horizon. A full rainbow emerged, extending from one end of the stage to the other. The crowd cheered at the beautiful symmetry.

Then, around 1,000 traditional folk drummers kicked off the inaugural piece. Their hands rose and fell on the stretched leather of the traditional drums at the same precise moment. The intensity was increasing with every second, elevating people's spirits and moods with every beat. With every thwack of the drum, the atmosphere seemed to become more and more charged.

As the drumming reached a crescendo, the skies split open. Rain and hail started coming down as if nature was feeling left out. Everyone was drenched from head to toe. The drummers welcomed nature's embrace and continued like an array of combustion engines, thrusting waves of energy into the charged atmosphere with their passionate drumming. The water on stage splashed under their feet as they stomped to the rhythm. The contrast was magical. My mind gave in, and I felt settled.

Delhi rains in the middle of March are as romantic as they are uncommon. Clearly, nobody came prepared with umbrellas or ponchos. Moments ago, people were waving flags from their countries. These flags were now repurposed as makeshift shelters. A drone shot would have captured a wet tapestry with a patchwork of colourful flags.

The surprise rains caused flooding everywhere. The riverbank's soil turned into mud under everyone's feet, making it very difficult to walk around without splattering muddy water on others. I could not believe that the Type-A New Yorker in me, who would get agitated when those careless yellow cabs would splash water as they drove by, was not only okay with this moment but was actually enjoying it.

By now, the rains had caused most of the LED screens to fuse. A good majority of the sound system had short-circuited. But that didn't dampen the enthusiasm of the crowd. Each performance would be welcomed and cheered, not only by the representatives from that country in the audience, but by everyone collectively. People appeared to be enveloped in a bubble of joy and belonging, tied together by an invisible thread.

It continued to rain, and I caught myself soaked in the moment. I felt like I had travelled back in time to when I was five years old and would run out of the house at the onset of the monsoon rains. I enjoyed splashing and jumping in the puddles, with specks of mud all over my clothes, not even sparing my face. And years later, here I was living it again, dancing on the muddy ground, completely drenched and with nothing to bother me. Banka and Alak were looking at each other, as if acknowledging their willing suspension of disbelief.

The massive starship-shaped stage spanned the area of seven football fields. A grand symphony of over 30,000 artists with 4,000 different instruments were now playing together. The entire stage wouldn't fit in my normal peripheral vision. Like trying to capture every action in a tennis match from courtside seats by the net, I had to move my head from side to side to even be able to see the proceedings on that massive stage, which stretched half a mile in length.

The next day, the entire organizing committee went up to Gurudev and requested that he change the venue to an indoor space. Gurudev asked them not to lose heart and to continue.

Over the next two days, various performances from all over the world continued on the mammoth stage. From Garba to Tango, Lithuanian folk dance to contemporary Sufi dance, German Polka and Shaolin Gongfu.

Many days ago . . .

Sri V, a dear friend of mine, was given the responsibility of coordinating the stage design and layout for the World Culture Festival. If that was not enough, she was also supposed to choreograph the finale dance routine with troops from over fifty countries, whom she would not have the chance to meet in-person until the evening before the event. Not overwhelming at all. She was in a huddle with other organizers and event planners, who were all collectively pulling their hair out while trying to get their arms around the scale of the event. She had a lot of doubts about how all of this was going to play out. No clear direction was emerging.

'Gurudev is calling for you.' Just then, a volunteer asked her to go see him. She stood impatiently in the corner, worrying until he called her.

'Haaan?' He called her closer with a hand gesture.

'I have seen it already. It is spectacular.' He said before Sri V could say anything, arresting her uncertainties and worries with a reassuring smile. And he stepped away before she could recover from what had just happened.

Gurudev had once laughingly said that the three most egotistical types in the world are artists, politicians and spiritual people—and here they were all sharing a stage. On stage were presidents and parliamentarians, artists from over 100 countries, spiritual leaders from the

Vatican, Imams from Syria and Iraq and various business leaders. And the diversity in the audience reflected that on the stage.

So many things could have gone wrong. Just one of them could have ruined everything. A new challenge appeared every other minute, and plans were changing constantly, not just until the last moment, but also during the event. And yet, it had all worked so beautifully. Despite all the mess, chaos, and obstacles, people were happily celebrating humanity. The volunteers not only saw the event through, but also stayed and cleaned the entire space afterwards, until the entire space was left better than it was found.

What was really working here was the power of intention. If an intention is strong enough, it can overcome the multitude of complications that we are all so skilled at creating.

Maharishi, a spiritual teacher from India, was responsible for driving the spiritual revolution in the US in the early 1960s. He was an enlightened master with a scientific approach, and he did a great service to humanity by spreading awareness about meditation and its benefits. The Maharishi Effect, a well-researched scientific phenomenon, has proven that even if 1per cent of the population meditates, it produces measurable improvements in the quality of life for the whole population. And here we were, just about 1 per cent of half the population of the world. While I had no device to measure the precise impact of this mass gathering on humanity, I walked away with a feeling that perhaps I was a part of something that positively shifted the collective consciousness of the planet.

Gurudev lead the sea of people in chanting the sound 'Om' together—which he describes as love and peace. Over 30,00,000 people took a long, deep breath in to say 'Om'. The vibrations filled up the skies. They felt so tangible. I too felt a little something in the cave of my heart. A collective intention was being sent out into the universe. An intention to let the peace within radiate around the world.

In 1981, soon after starting the Art of Living, Gurudev went into a period of silence with the intention to bring peace to every heart, a smile on every face and a tangible experience of connecting with the Self. During this time, Sudarshan Kriya (SKY) came to him as a poem. The uber intelligent consciousness revealed its song to him.

Vibrations of 'Om' persisted in air like a slow-moving, rain-bearing cloud. The atmosphere went back to stillness. There was not even a faint ripple in this sea of people, meditating on the bank of a river.

He Is That

People don't get me. Sometimes, even I don't get me. But
you get me all the time. I can't deny it anymore. I can only
treasure it like the sunset. After all, all I know is that when
you know, you know.

It is like listening to Miles Davis' jazz. You can feel the
magnanimity and grandeur of the music in your bones,
but you just can't tell where it's coming from. And when
you can't use your intellect to unpack it, you just drop the
intellect altogether. Drop the effort to understand it fully
and lose yourself in the thick forest of masterfully arranged
musical notes that create a tickle up your spine.

I had begun traveling with Gurudev as much as I
could. Banka would accompany Alak and I on most of our
trips. We observed Gurudev closely, only to realize that the
more I got to know about him, the less I understood him.
A few years ago, I would never have accepted the defeat of

my mighty mind in trying to figure out this phenomenon. But in this case, I still had no idea how deep the rabbit hole continued.

And yet, to my surprise, I was in acceptance. I could never have imagined my analytical left brain to be comfortable with not being in control. Nor could I have ever imagined it to drop its questioning and judgemental nature. But somehow, there was no feverish desire to figure it all out. There was no rush, and no false sense of urgency—something I had fought with all my life.

Every time I brought up my wonderment about how I was okay with not being in control to Banka, he would smile gently and high-five me.

One of my favourite authors, George Orwell, once said that to see what is in front of one's nose requires constant struggle. I had experienced this. But now my struggle was over. I was experiencing something magnanimous. I had been seeking this for a long time. Perhaps for lifetimes.

Many years ago, some of us had embarked upon a hiking trip in Torres Del Paine, a mystical landscape located at the southern tip of Chile. One evening, we began walking on a narrow trail that passed through the thick forest. A park ranger discouraged us from proceeding, but we figured that just a few more hours would get us to our destination. Anyway, it didn't get dark until closer to midnight in that part of the world. The terrain for first half an hour was deceptively flat, dotted with white daisies. Soon enough, it began showing its true colours. The daisies vanished. The ground beneath our feet started rising steeply. The wind began gusting at forty miles per hour. With heavy backpacks on our shoulders, we were being flung around. We slowed down significantly.

The more I travelled with Gurudev, the more I watched him, the more I meditated with him, the more I internalized his wisdom, the more privileged I felt to have a living master.

It was slowly morphing into a relationship like none other. I enjoyed being around him. Soaking in his presence. Learning from him. Nothing else brought me as much joy and fulfilment. In every difficult situation that I found myself in, I had imagined how the master would handle it. It would instantly bring me so much clarity and relief. And it never got old or boring. There was just so much newness along every step of the way.

And then we hit the marshlands. The land beneath our feet turned mushy. We slowed down. The light was fading now and so were the signs of the trail amidst the wet ground. We reached a place that looked very familiar—we had been there half an hour ago. We were now going in circles, and it was almost dark. Frustrations hit an all-time high as our spirits fell to an all-time low. We had been warned not to be in the forest at night to avoid encounters with wild Pumas. Nervous and disheartened, we looked at each other's faces, drowning in darkness and worry. Going back wasn't an option. So, we prayed to the universe and continued walking. Within a few minutes, the entire forest became a shade brighter, and then another shade brighter. It was as if someone was approaching fast with a powerful torch light from behind. We turned around to see.

For the longest time, I kept fighting with the big scary creatures in life as well as on the spiritual path. But it was all a making of my own mind. Like gruesome looming shadows on the wall. And now that I had turned towards the light, the shadows had disappeared. Even if they were still there, I didn't care.

As we turned around, we saw the most magnanimous moon of our lives. All this time it had been there, hidden behind the clouds. And now it was shining in its full glory, peeking over the shoulders of the Andes mountains in the distance. It was a sight to behold. I had never witnessed anything like that before. It was shining on us through its blemishes. In the most unanticipated manner, nature got us back on the trail.

All this time, there had been an invisible force nudging me to do the right thing. A steady source of light. At times so obvious and at times hidden behind my cloudy mind. Sometimes showing me the right direction, and sometimes holding my hand until I reached the destination. Gurudev was my spiritual guide. My mentor. My Master. With a capital M. And I felt a thrill, having him by my side on the winding trail of life. With that guiding light, why would I be deterred from walking into the thick forest of the unknown?

IV

Strange Are the Ways of a Master

If you think you are dull, your Guru is brilliant.
If you think you are brilliant, your Guru is irrational.
If you think you are irrational, your Guru is irresistible.
If you complain, your Guru gets tougher.
If you are perfect, your Guru is imperfection personified.
Do you still want to have a Guru?
It is inviting all sorts of trouble!

—Gurudev

The Wonder Years

I sometimes forget that Gurudev wasn't always the person I see before me today as the master. He was also a child once. Then a young man. But my mind can barely entertain the thought that he was anything other than what he is right now. How was his childhood? What was his path? Who was his master?

Gurudev was born in the small village of Papanasam, Tamil Nadu, in southern India. He was born on a Sunday. He also shared his birthday with Adi Shankaracharya, a renowned saint from early eighth century. Hence, his parents named him Ravi Shankar.

There was something undeniably different about little Ravi's presence, and everyone had begun to notice that he was not an ordinary child.

His parents began to witness unusual behaviour from Ravi. At a very young age, he showed a keen interest in ancient wisdom & philosophy. At the tender age of four, he could recite entire verses of the Bhagwad Gita, an ancient scripture.

His parents would often find him gazing far into the horizon in a contemplative state or sitting in deep meditation.

His interests as a child were very different from children his age.

Several mystics had said that he was no ordinary child and urged his parents not to bind him to the material world. They had predicted that he would go on to become an enlightened being, uplifting millions of people around the world. It was all a little too intangible for his friends and family to entertain, and it certainly managed to scare the living daylights out of Ravi's mother.

After one such visit from a renowned saint, who echoed these sentiments, a storm of emotions overtook his mother.

'Will you give up everything and become a monk one day, Ravi?' She murmured, struggling in vain to hold back her tears. Her heart was heavy in anticipation of losing him.

Ravi went up to her and wrapped his little arms around her.

'I will never ever leave you Amma, please don't cry,' he whispered—a promise he kept until the end.

By the time he was a teenager, it became apparent that his life was heading towards something very different. While others were living a normal teenage life, he began teaching meditation. People around him could not understand why.

'What does he do after all, sitting all day holding his nose?' They would squarely disapprove of his breath work and meditation practice.

'Get a legit job instead,' they'd say.

It must have been difficult to grow up as an outlier in a world that wants one to be close to the mean of normal distribution. To remain misunderstood is perhaps the price one pays to be a nonconformist.

So, he went to find a job.

'What do you do?' asked the first interviewer in a somewhat dismissive tone.

'I teach meditation.'

This peaked the collective curiosity of all three interviewers on the panel.

'Tell us more about it,' one of them said.

'Maybe you can teach us how to meditate, too.' The interviewer's tone had become soft and warm.

For the next two days, Ravi Shankar taught them breathing and meditation.

This is how his first and last job interview played out. He was simply not interested.

Enter Maharishi.

I had read about Maharishi Mahesh Yogi and his path while I was reading up on Gurudev early on. Gurudev had spent a lot of his formative years with Maharishi. Some believed he was Gurudev's teacher. Some told me otherwise. I was curious.

Maharishi made meditation a household term. He scooped it out of the corners of consciousness and made it accessible to humanity. He put that which is unexplainable into a simple modern technique— Transcendental Meditation (TM). In the late 1960s and early 1970s, Maharishi was the rock star of meditation with the Beatles, Beach Boys and other celebrities as his followers.

'Maharishi touched the lives of millions. He transformed free-thinking hippies of the sixties into meditators and people with a constrained material outlook to yogis shining with confidence and brilliance. He raised the state of mind of those who were desperate and depressed to those who were hopeful of getting enlightened.' Gurudev once said about Maharishi.

Ravi Shankar went on to spend some time with Maharishi in his late teens and early twenties. He also studied Vedic literature at the Maharishi European Research Institute (MERU) in Seelisberg, Switzerland. Maharishi had established MERU in order to encourage research into the field of consciousness. Ravi Shankar invested several years working side by side with Maharishi. It was a relationship full of mutual respect and love.

Maharishi adored and respected Gurudev, or Ravi back then. He wanted Ravi to be the Shankaracharya—a Sanskrit name for the one who presides on the seat of knowledge—and entrusted him with the highest level of responsibility. Gurudev was the heir apparent of the prolific TM movement.

Then, one day, at the pinnacle of his journey within the TM movement, young Ravi Shankar gave it all up and started the Art of Living.

To understand the dynamics between Gurudev and Maharishi, I spoke to several wise men who have been involved for a long time. Just as every shaft of a tunnel leads to two or three more openings in a labyrinth, every time I learned something about Maharishi and Gurudev, it created more questions in turn.

I have always cheered for people who take the road less travelled. Hence, I had newfound respect for Gurudev when I learned about him carving his own path. It felt strangely relatable. My applause, however, was interrupted in the very next moment by a flood of questions that appeared in my head. Why did he leave Maharishi? Did he get bored of doing the same thing for years?

Dealing with Boredom

I am reminded of a particularly warm afternoon in Boone, NC. The Art of Living Retreat Centre overlooks an expansive valley, contained on the other side by the majestic Blue Ridge mountains. Just past the meditation hall, there is a large opening through the canopy of leafy trees that looks out at the mountains.

Gurudev usually meets with visitors and volunteers in a small living room. That day, the room was full of people. His last meeting had just ended, and he was casually chatting with someone. I was standing in the corner, hoping to meet with Gurudev soon.

Gurudev looked in my direction. Our eyes met and he greeted me with a warm smile.

'Have you read what I wrote on boredom years ago?' He asked me out of nowhere.

'I haven't, Gurudev. Where can I find it?' I responded. I wondered why he had asked me, out of everyone sitting in the room. Did I look bored out of my mind? I had never had a conversation with him on that matter.

He rooted out a piece of paper from underneath a bunch of letters given to him by people.

'Read this loudly so that everyone can hear,' he told me. Every single eye in the room was suddenly on me. Banka was silently smiling at me from the corner nearby. 'Don't mess it up!' He was saying, without using any words.

'Are you ever bored?' The first line of the article opened with a question. Yes! This was for me. I told myself.

'The question of a young boy kept ringing in my mind—am I ever bored? Perhaps a question that had never crossed my mind.'

This was the exact question I've had for him for quite some time now! I was tempted to scan the remainder of the letter quickly to see if there was a simple yes or no somewhere in there. Instead, I continued to read Gurudev's writing aloud.

I look out the window. The waves unceasingly washing the shore—are these waves bored? The clouds—are they bored? And I, who am watching them, not bored. I go on to analyzing . . . Boredom is stagnation, but nothing in life seems to be stagnant. You are not bored when you are asleep or when you are fully awake, or when you are awake to the ever-changing scenario.

I try to get bored looking at the ocean with the tranquil green water, the shimmering rays of sun . . . Suppose if everything stops, if everything stands still, will I be bored? A certain silence dawns, a presence overtaking. The answer was loud and clear: no! The changes cannot bore you for they don't let you feel the time. And when you feel the time, everything stands still—including your mind. Perhaps it is the restlessness in the mind that creates the boredom. When you are still, there is no restlessness. When you are dynamic, there is no restlessness . . . I go on analyzing.

I paused momentarily. I wanted to take a break and go back to reading it again. I wanted to think more about restlessness in mind and movement. But people around me wanted me to keep going.

Then I open the window. A gush of air rushes in, knocking down the vase and the picture on the table and all the tiny objects Mary had placed there. In a moment, everything is on the floor and the room looks wrecked and in a mess. Did it make a difference? I watched . . . Did it make any difference? To me, not one bit. Perhaps someone in the place would be upset. I tried to put myself in Mary's shoes and see. Would she be upset? Her smiling face comes across. I cannot imagine.

She was so excited to have me as a guest in her home for the weekend. The love and sparks in her eyes said it. She was prepared to do anything to have the pleasure of being a hostess. Would she be upset?

I pick up the mess, but I cannot do anything about the silken carpet and the floor that is one-third wet. In life, we can change certain things; certain things we need to accept. It is only time that can fix them—or not fix them at all.

I go back to the window. The ocean is the same, unruffled by the mess in the room. I am the same. I can stand there for a million years. I would not get bored. I wouldn't want a change; nor would I mind a change.

Right then, a sailboat floats on the water. I think of how our bodies are like boats afloat on the ocean of existence. I am the boat on the ocean. The boat has moved; I look at the mirror; the body has changed. The picture of me that Mary has on her table looks different. I had more hair then. It used to take half an hour to comb my hair. Now it takes less than three minutes. Yet I am the same: no change, no growth, no boredom, no nothing . . .

I pick up the snack—the 'no-nothing' stuff left on the table for me—'no wheat, no fat, no sugar . . .' the list goes on. No taste! I burst into laughter. It reminds me of Adi Shankara, 'I am not the body, not the mind, not the intellect, not the ego . . .'

'These layers of identification have clouded the being. The being . . . washed like the ocean. Deep inside we are all untouched, soaking in the being. Soaked in it, there is no boredom, there is no depression. I feel like shouting at the top of my voice from the Eiffel Tower, "Hey, wake up! You are bubbling joy! Be free! Would anyone hear me?"'

I hear you Gurudev. Loud and clear. But sometimes life takes over. What do I do?

'I hear a knock on the door. Mary and a few others stand there with fruits. I drape myself with the shawl and welcome them. I feel like apologizing . . . I tell them I made a mess of the room. They don't ask me why or how. Nor do I explain. They seem to be overjoyed to be able to clean up, to get to spend some time in the room.

'If the daughter had left such a mess, would it be the same?'

'Does it read *the* daughter or *her* daughter?' Gurudev interrupted me. He had noticed that my tongue slipped.

'Sorry, my bad,' I apologized and continued. Not just me, but the entire room full of people, had noticed his awareness.

If her daughter had left such a mess, would it be the same?

The big 'Why?' makes us angry about the past? It can even lead to violence. We can only criticize or take criticism with a smile when the deep sense of belongingness is there. When one feels connected, feels the love, the words do not bring up anger.

In life, it is meaningless to go into such inquiries. Just, 'What can I do to bring order?' If you are not shaken by the mess and chaos, you can act and do something about it. Our smile unshaken, our conviction strong, we can clean up any mess in our life.

The room fell silent. My mind went completely blank.

He looked at my shocked expression and blinked his eyes with a smile.

My questioning mind had settled.

I left the kutir happy as a clam on high water with the precious piece of paper in my hands.

He Was the Teacher Who Never Was

While pursuing his bachelor of science, one day, a corner of a local newspaper caught Ravi Shankar's eye. Maharishi's organization in Bangalore had announced a programme on the Science of Creative Intelligence.

The little ad in the newspaper promised to provide a practical means to unfold the permanent experience of higher states of consciousness. I wondered how esoteric it may have appeared back then, when meditation and yoga were for people who were 'so out there'.

As a student of physics, Ravi Shankar was naturally curious about the connection between science and spirituality, and so, he enrolled for the program. These classes were conducted long-distance on a colour television—a novelty in those days. Ravi—as he was addressed by his classmates—enjoyed the program and looked forward to meeting with Maharishi, whom he had seen only on the TV screen thus far.

After the program, an opportunity arose for Ravi Shankar to go and meet with Maharishi in Trichur, a town 300 miles southwest of Bangalore. But as fate would have it, he could not meet Maharishi during that trip. Maharishi had somehow come to know about him by then. 'Is that boy there?' He would ask people around him.

One evening, Maharishi was flying out of Kochi, the closest town to Trichur with an airport. Ravi Shankar set off to Kochi to meet Maharishi at the airport. And once again, due to an unfortunate sequence of events, he could not meet him.

One day, Ravi Shankar received a call inviting him to come meet Maharishi in Rishikesh. His excitement at meeting Maharishi was unmistakable. As his sister Bhanu later recounted, at that time, nobody in her family knew that their lives were soon going to transform completely. This was the year 1975. Gurudev was nineteen.

Ravi Shankar arrived in Rishikesh to meet with Maharishi in his ashram. Years later, in an attempt to trace the path of history, I would follow Gurudev's footsteps to the same place.

'The first thing I noticed was Maharishi's sandals outside the door,' said Gurudev. He waited outside before he was asked in. As he entered the room, Maharishi greeted him with an affectionate smile.

'He looked at me warmly. He recognized me and I recognized him,' Gurudev said.

After returning from Rishikesh, Ravi Shankar spent a few days at home before moving to Switzerland. He would spend the next couple of years with Maharishi as a student of Vedic literature. Those were Gurudev's formative years.

While Maharishi and Gurudev shared the most beautiful relationship, he never accepted Ravi Shankar as his student.

Ravi Shankar once asked Maharishi if he could initiate him through Diksha—a traditional consecration ceremony given one-to-one by the master to the student. Diksha is considered to be the beginning of a lifelong commitment to the spiritual path and symbolizes the minds of the teacher and the student becoming one. Maharishi simply avoided that conversation.

In the Vedic teacher–student tradition, it is customary for a student to offer salutations to the teacher by reverentially bowing down. However, Maharishi never allowed him to do that either.

Maharishi would always offer Ravi Shankar a seat right next to him. Playing with the word Ravi—meaning the sun in Sanskrit—Maharishi would say, 'When the sun will rise, there will be light everywhere and the veil of ignorance will disappear.'

With time, Maharishi started to entrust Ravi Shankar with more and more responsibilities, sending him to various *mutts* (monasteries) to represent him. He kept delegating more and more work to Ravi Shankar, who was barely in his early twenties then.

It continued to baffle me why Maharishi would not accept such a sincere seeker as his student.

Ravi Shankar's rising importance in the organization and Maharishi's attention on him had sparked jealousy amongst fellow colleagues. Some would try to slow him down, and often created obstacles in his work. Even the spiritual path is not free from competition and envy.

Maharishi wanted Ravi Shankar to be the Shankaracharya of Puri, the heritage city in the state of Odisha in eastern India. This was a huge honour, as the Puri monastery is one of the four cardinal monasteries established in the eighth century. So Maharishi sent him to Puri.

'I didn't want to wear saffron clothes and remain stuck in one place. I had a vision that my work was waiting for me all over the world,' said Gurudev.

Years ago, young Ravi Shankar's parents were puzzled by such statements. Ravi would tell the other children in school that he had family all over the world, and soon he would travel abroad to see them. His mother would rebuke him for lying. Little did she know.

Ravi Shankar respectfully declined the Shankaracharya seat that was coveted by many.

In the summer of 1983, Gurudev was at a railway station in Hubli. He was on a platform with tickets for two different trains: one northward bound to Sholapur and the other southward bound to Bengaluru. The Sholapur-bound train would lead him to start a movement of his own. The Bengaluru-bound train would take him back to TM.

'One of the most difficult decisions I have had to make was to leave Maharishi and embark upon the journey to start the Art of Living Foundation,' Gurudev said when I asked him how he finally decided to take such a monumental step.

Leaving Maharishi was painful, especially since his departure occurred at a time when a lot of people were leaving. It was as if there was an exodus away from the movement.

On the one hand, Gurudev had the honour and responsibility of perpetuating Maharishi's entire life's work. On the other hand, he could feel that millions of people were waiting for him. He would have visions of the large Art of Living gatherings and the millions of people waiting for him to eventually walk the path through the Art of Living Foundation.

Which train to board? The one going north or the one going south?

'I took a step forward and my feet effortlessly turned towards the Sholapur-bound train,' said Gurudev.

Once in a while, life presents everyone with defining choices. And there is such a complex mechanism behind what makes one choose what they choose.

Once, at a gathering in Santa Monica back in the eighties, someone asked Gurudev what his mission was.

'I have no mission,' came the earnest response.

To that end, he never had a master plan—at least not on paper. In contrast, Maharishi always had a formal plan. He would have a seven-year plan for spiritual regeneration of the planet. One could read it and track the progress. Gurudev's approach was quite the opposite.

I have interacted with most of the people who had been part of Gurudev's journey since the beginning of the Art of Living in the US. After all, there were only a handful to begin with. They all have one thing in common. Whatever they were doing at that time felt special, and yet no one had any inkling where it was all headed.

I was gradually beginning to appreciate the bond between Gurudev and Maharishi. Gurudev had chosen to walk a less comfortable path in order to serve the greater good. And yet, there was no element of stopping one journey and starting another. There was no transition. It was a smooth continuum simply facilitated by the invisible hand of creation.

I imagined Maharishi standing at a bend of a river, and Gurudev standing downstream by the same river. A river that is both ancient and new at the same time.

Love Me Do

My father and I puffed our way to the top of the cliff in Rishikesh, to what used to be Maharishi's old ashram. To the locals, it's known as the Beatles' ashram. The influential young rock stars descended upon this ashram to learn meditation with Maharishi back in the 1960s. My trip to Rishikesh wouldn't be complete if I didn't visit this place where two iconic forces of nature—one that I loved and one that I respected—came together.

Far in the distance, the azure waters of the Ganga were flowing like an intense pirouette, dancing away to the music in her own head. What used to be a thriving meditation haven not too long ago, now appeared to be a mere shell of its former self. Life-size murals and groovy artwork adorned the walls, creating a photo-op for tourists. However, in my heart, I felt a sense of pain when seeing the decrepit structures that these paintings were unsuccessfully trying to mask. Silenced by time, the abandoned and dilapidated buildings were trying to convey the eternal truth of life, how everything is constantly changing. The walls were standing there as witness.

We walked down towards the main meditation hall, and along the way, I noticed a blue sign that said 'Ved Bhavan'. It immediately transported me to an evening in Canada when Gurudev shared a funny story from the time he had spent in this very ashram with Maharishi.

Once, on a moonlit evening, Gurudev was taking a walk with Maharishi and four others in the ashram. It was a sort of routine, where Maharishi discussed ideas and delegated work as they walked. As they approached the flower garden, Maharishi very casually suggested that they build a huge structure—the Ved Bhavan—right there. The building would primarily be used for the study of Vedic scriptures.

'Let's begin right now,' he announced. The construction crew was woken up at midnight. Somebody started taking measurements for the foundation. Markings for pillars were made. There was a mature, leafy tree on one edge of the garden, and someone even started uprooting it. Complete chaos ensued.

Gurudev suggested waiting until the following day and consulting an engineer. But the idea fell on deaf ears. Digging for the foundation had already started and no one was in a mood to listen. Many times, I have observed how the evolved logical minds of some of the smartest people I've known cease while in the presence of a spiritual master. Why should it be any different then?

The colours of the flowers to be planted on each floor became quite an involved topic of discussion—in the middle of the night! Someone wanted brightly coloured flowers, while others wanted all-season flowers.

Suddenly, the moon disappeared behind a thick veil of dark clouds. It started drizzling, and the haphazard construction work came to a standstill. Perhaps it was nature's way of restoring balance. Nature brings equilibrium in odd ways. You cannot touch something without being touched.

The next morning, many people were in complete shock as they had no idea why the beautiful flower garden had been completely decimated. Eventually, an engineer ruled out the possibility of a structure in that place, as the undercurrent of the Ganga would eventually destroy the foundation. And that was that.

At a distance, I heard a man strumming his guitar and singing a Beatles' tune that was written and composed on this very campus.

Words are flowing out like endless rain into a paper cup,
They slither while they pass, they slip away across the universe,
Pools of sorrow, waves of joy are drifting through my open mind,

Possessing and caressing me . . .
Jai Gurudeva Om
Nothing's gonna change my world . . .

Today, the Ved Bhavan sits on the opposite side of the ashram, away from the river. A structure that was built with so much enthusiasm and planning, now stands abandoned.

That day, Gurudev told me something that has stayed with me.

'If all your experiences can be explained logically, then you have missed something very important in life.' Gurudev said, before I could even ask him about how such a group of intellectuals didn't think before jumping in. The timing of what he said was so surreal that it felt as if he was reading my mind like a book.

I was naturally drawn towards the singer. He was sitting with his back resting on a white wall, on which were inscribed three familiar words in big red font— Jai Guru Dev.

My mind wandered to a warm, breezy afternoon in Buenos Aires. The Argentine duo of the So What Project! had just activated their electric guitars and kicked off their peppy number 'Krishna Govinda' in a boost of high-octane energy. A total of 1,50,000 Argentinians had gathered for one of the largest mass meditations on the planet. Gurudev was walking along the long ramp—which extended to the centre of the park—waving at the crowd. The end of his shawl swept the floor behind him while his hair blew in all directions, as if the wind couldn't make up its mind in the excitement.

Just a few minutes ago, the entire park had been still. One could hear a pin drop as Gurudev lead the crowd in a meditation. A good majority of those gathered there didn't speak English, and most of them were meeting him for the first time.

The crowd was thrilled as he began to speak to them in his broken Spanish.

The ramp extended nearly half a kilometre into the audience. An aerial shot from a drone was projected onto the screens. There was not one open space as far as the eye could see. Far in the distance, installed on a platform about six high were three gigantic white letters—J G D.

'Jai Guru Dev!'

The very first time I was greeted with these words was by an usher at one of the meditation events in Metuchen, NJ. Later, I realized everyone in Art of Living greeted each other with these three words, like some secret password needed to enter a back-alley poker club. It was an awkward moment to say the least. I think I just mumbled good evening and smiled back. This person must have experienced one of those moments where you extend your hand for a handshake, and the other person responds with folded hands in Namaste. I couldn't really decide what made me more uncomfortable—the greeting or the usher's unrestrained enthusiasm in taking me to my seat. 'He is just trying to show you your place,' Alak laughed out loud.

My drifting mind was brought back to the present moment by my father who was now waving at me from a distance. I moved away from the guitarist, and as I was leaving, he smiled and said, 'Jai Guru Dev.' I nodded with a smile and responded with the same greeting. This time the words come out effortlessly.

What lead to my initial discomfort with this phrase was that I thought it referred to 'Gurudev' being, well, Gurudev. It somehow reminded me of many self-proclaimed, fame-seeking, money-minded, so-called gurus in India. And I must admit, I also thought that it was self-promotional.

So, what changed?

Turns out I should have been asking, 'What is Gurudev?' instead of 'Who is Gurudev?'

While flipping through some insights shared by Gurudev in his younger days, I came across this transcription:

Jai Guru Dev is victory to the Big Mind in you that is both dignified and playful. That is what Jai Guru Dev means: 'Victory to the Greatness in you.'

As if one mind was not enough, now I had to learn to deal with two minds! How were they really different? I thought the big mind and small mind just had anatomical differences, but then I was never a good biology student.

The small mind is the chatty guy in your life, constantly seeking attention. Most of the time, he's getting himself in trouble. There are more than seven billion small minds. One per person. The Big Mind, on the other hand, is like the cool guy chilling at the back of the bar, who effortlessly attracts women, much to the envy of all the other guys who secretly wish they could be him, but don't know how.

The small mind is our individual consciousness. It is like the wave on the surface of the Big Mind. When the turbulence in the small mind quietens down, it merges with the universal consciousness, the Big Mind. Just like the choppy wave ceases to exist in the depths of the big ocean. Jai Guru Dev—the victory of that which is in you, and also in me.

Once, I happened to be with Gurudev in the Canadian ashram. It was time for bed. Gurudev generally sleeps on the floor. Except, in this room, there was a raised wooden platform that was almost twice the height of a normal bed. Gurudev shared the quirky incident behind it. His room, on the second floor of a small wooden house, overlooks a body of water. Gurudev had asked the construction person to see if he could bring the window down a bit, so that he could watch the water at eye level. Apparently, the construction fellow couldn't figure out how to move the window down, so he raised the bed instead. We all joined Gurudev in hearty laughter as he shared the incident. With the raised wooden platform and a small chair in the corner, there was not much space in the room. There was a picture of Maharishi smiling on the ledge of one of the windows.

'Let's go around the world,' Gurudev said as he closed his eyes to meditate. The four of us in the room sat on the floor around him. The lights were dimmed. I was familiar with this end-of-the-day routine, but I didn't really know what happened in there. Gurudev closed his eyes and then started off. I had no idea who he met with, healed, hugged, or high-fived. Like Maharishi had delegated work to the four on the walk that evening, I wondered if Gurudev would give us some responsibilities on this nocturnal trip.

I didn't know how long the meditation lasted. I had lost complete awareness.

'Jai Guru Dev,' Gurudev whispered as he concluded. The room was pulsating with energy.

With thoughts of the Big Mind churning in my small mind, I managed to catch up with my father. He was staring at the meditation caves built on the edge of the cliff, overlooking the Ganga. These standalone caves were built to provide seclusion for the meditators. I really wanted to go in and meditate, just to experience the energy of those before me. But we had a flight to catch.

The setting sun glistening on the distant, playful Ganga and the guitarist leaning on the white wall were immersed in the stillness of time. He was now humming and strumming to the Beatles' 'Love me Do', and the Big Mind was soaking in the love of that rich and unforgettable moment.

Travelling Light

Two old suitcases gathering dust in the attic of my parents' home in India are all that is left of my grandparents' and great grandparents' life journeys. No longer used or even usable, with their all-metal bodies and rusty joints, they survive as family relics. They are completely non-functional, but at some level are also my only connection with previous generations, and for some odd reason, I don't even feel like throwing the suitcases away. Much like some of the baggage I carry in my own mind.

I stood there impatiently, waiting for my baggage to show up as part of an array of things appearing sequentially from the scanning machine. I wish I could also watch my own mind like a scanning machine—a quiet witness to everything that passes through it without being affected—but still have the intelligence to discriminate what is good and what is not.

A familiar face surprised me. 'I thought you were flying out tomorrow?' I asked Brian, who was busy hobbling past the security checkpoint at Charlotte airport.

'I sure am.' Brian winked and dashed towards the gates. He had no bags with him. I would later discover that he had bought a cheap ticket to somewhere he hadn't planned to go, just to get past security so that he could spend some time with Gurudev before he boarded his flight to Washington DC.

Walking towards the gate in giddy excitement, my mind flashed back to my first trip with Gurudev.

Usually there is a formal approval process one has to go through in order to travel with Gurudev, given the sheer number of people wanting to do so. Two of my dear friends had gone through the official process and had been planning for quite some time to travel with Gurudev. They happened to mention it to me a week before their trip. I wanted to do many things in life, but until then, travelling with a guru had never been on my list.

Without much thought, however, Banka and I jumped in. Unfortunately, Alak couldn't join. Of course, I had taken no official permissions and broken all the protocols. So, I was a little concerned about how it would all play out.

'These angels have come from far. Take good care of them.' Gurudev told the admin person looking after the quaint ashram located under the pine-serrated skies of the Black Forest in Germany. I was overjoyed, like a gate-crashing teenager who had made it past the velvet ropes. I really didn't expect him to say that.

The next morning, Banka and I were loitering outside Gurudev's room on the second floor, wondering what could possibly be going on behind the closed doors. The usual faces seen around Gurudev were nowhere in sight, so I imagined everyone must be inside.

'Let's just go inside,' Banka suggested. Feeling part anxious, part curious, and part left out, I gathered my courage to enter the room. The door opened easily, and I tiptoed in like the Pink Panther. Banka followed quietly. To my surprise, it was just Gurudev and us. For a moment, I felt out of place. A set of mixed feelings overcame me—a bout of giddy excitement and nervousness to be in the same room as him. He was on the phone by the window. Was I invading his privacy? For a moment I felt like leaving, but my feet didn't move. I stood motionless in a corner not knowing what to do. My body was still, but my mind was running around like a three-month old Labrador puppy that had just awoken from a long nap.

I began scanning the spartan but well-lit room. There was not much furniture, except for a couple of chairs. No bed either. Just a thin mattress on the floor by the window.

What was I doing really doing in there? What should I talk to him about? This was perhaps my opportunity to ask him all the big questions I have always had. But maybe I had no business asking him any questions. My track record for listening to his advice wasn't anything to write home about. My mind was both buzzing and empty at the same time. I tried to think of something intelligible. Banka couldn't hold back his laughter at my predicament. It made me even more queasy.

Gurudev finished the phone conversation and turned around. He smiled at me.

'Haan? What do you want to ask?' He chuckled.

Wait, did he just scan my thoughts? Oh no. I hope he didn't peek into my thoughts from an hour ago.

'I'm fine, Gurudev. How are you?' Wait. What did I just say? I couldn't believe the incoherent bunch of words that had managed to escape my mouth. So much for a refined and intellectual line of questioning.

I reached the gate at Charlotte airport to find that there were about sixty people crowded around Gurudev. There were, however, only a handful of us who were actually travelling with him. Even though all this may appear circumstantial to the unsuspecting, it hardly ever is.

The crowd giggled and swathed around with a singular purpose. Gurudev was mindful of the inconveniences that may be caused to fellow travellers by the group. He found himself a quiet corner while we waited for the boarding process to begin. Nobody wanted to miss the opportunity to walk up to him and get a private audience for a few moments. Gurudev took a seat and the chair next to him instantaneously turned into the most desirable real estate. In a silent game of musical chairs, the pack descended upon it one-by-one. After a brief conversation and perhaps a selfie, the seat's inhabitant would reluctantly make way for the next person eagerly waiting for their turn.

Many were handing him letters. Some were scribbling away on scraps of paper. Gurudev patiently accepted every single piece of paper, including carefully folded Starbucks napkins from the less prepared.

Throughout my first trip to Germany, people kept giving him letters wherever he went. A somewhat similar wave of affection as the present day. One night, he passed me a stack of letters. I didn't know what to do. He gave no instructions. So, I just started taking them out of envelopes one after the other and arranging them neatly for him to read later. I assumed I was supposed to do that.

'Tell her she can come to Bangalore in August,' came instructions from the guru. He was pacing around the room with a determined stride. Tell who? I was perplexed. My experienced friend, who also happened to be in the room, hinted to me with his eyes to open the sealed envelope in my hands. I sliced it open and found a handwritten note in barely legible handwriting. The woman who wrote the note was asking Gurudev when she could come see him in India.

This continued for some time. 'Letters from Art of Living teachers in another pile,' he would say. Then I'd open the envelope and find a letter in Polish and some broken English, written by an Art of Living instructor from Warsaw. How did he do it? More so, why was he even making me do this? I felt the letters did not need to be opened and sorted by me.

The boarding announcement at Charlotte airport disrupted my stream of thoughts. Gurudev got up to go. The crowd still didn't seem to want to leave him, so they also inched their way toward the gate. Gurudev smiled and signalled for them to stay back, so that other passengers were not hassled. Banka signalled to me by squeezing his otherwise curious eyes as if someone had squirted lemon juice in them. He asked me, without speaking, to grab the good old yellow Asana from the chair that Gurudev stood up from.

On that same trip to Germany, Banka had similarly signalled to me to pick up Gurudev's unfolded silk kaftan from the chair in his room, by squeezing his otherwise curious eyes. I had picked it up and started folding. The cloth was too delicate, and by the time I got to the one corner, the fine fabric had already fallen off from the other corner fold. I tried again, and this time the fabric from the centre fold came off.

'You American boy!'

Gurudev laughed at me and took the cloth from my hands. Then with a swift movement of his hands, he perfectly folded that tricky piece of cloth. And then tossed it back at me, only for it to disintegrate again. I kept thinking how my mind is equally as delicate and tricky to handle. For some others, not so much.

I picked up the Asana and folded it in the first attempt. Luckily, it wasn't made of silk.

As I inched my way towards the front of the line, a long and drawn-out yawn escaped my mouth. The fatigue of the last several days had begun to surface, and suddenly, even something as uncomfortable as a cramped airline seat seemed appealing. On my last trip with Gurudev, we had zipped around across the US and Canada, visiting thirteen cities in less than three weeks. I noticed that he barely slept for three to four hours a day. First, I thought it was an anomaly. He must have been jet-lagged, I thought. I realized only later, after speaking with many others, that it was a norm for him. Towards the end of that trip, I was completely exhausted, while he was as fresh as a daisy. At each destination, his day would be packed with meetings with a wide range of individuals—government officials, war veterans, teachers, scientists, artists, people with problems, people without problems . . . and the list went on. And the scenery at each airport was not much different from this one. He moved like an accelerated particle with agility and energy that defied the classical laws of motion. How did he do it all and still not look tired? I went up to him and asked him what his secret was. I could use it too.

'Well, that is my nature! When you follow your nature, there is no conflict, no confusion. Just clarity and action,' he responded.

Just before boarding, the attendant asked me to check my bag at the gate as the overhead bins in the main cabin were full. Perhaps this was the universe telling me to drop my baggage and relax in the space within.

Gurudev stepped on to the aerobridge, turned around, smiled, and waved at the crowd one last time. The send-off party erupted in multitudes of goodbyes. Some were emotional and teary-eyed. Some were delighted about the time they had been able to spend with him. Some were on the tips of their toes, stretching their necks out to wave one last time before he disappeared into the aircraft. They were all at the same sweet spot—in the present moment. Everyone seemed to have dropped their baggage in that moment.

And off he went, onwards with his journey—also the destination.

A Story of Success. A Story of Failure.

Later that summer, I was planning my travels with Gurudev. Little did I know how eventful that trip would turn out to be.

Gaston Hall of historic Georgetown University in Washington DC, was unusually packed for a Sunday afternoon. It had red carpets, oak wood-panelled walls that were intricately carved and painted, decorated wooden ceilings, and a series of classical allegorical paintings adorning the walls. Remove the stage, install a pulpit, and the entire hall could pass for an ornate nineteenth-century church. The stage was bare except for two comfortable-looking chairs.

The walls of the hall bore the names of intellectual stalwarts of various fields. My eyes rested on 'LaGrange', an Italian mathematician who lived in France and impacted the world through his work. He was someone I had admired, studied and by now, almost forgotten.

How knowledge travels without barriers! On the wall was an oil painting of Athena—the goddess of wisdom. She seemed to nod in agreement.

I was comfortably settled in the fifth row. Many presidents, eminent leaders, and heads of state have spoken in this hall. In my recent memory, I recalled President Obama's speech from this very location. Very soon, Gurudev would be here. The lights dimmed. Following a fetching introduction, Gurudev walked on to the stage amidst roaring applause.

'Are you all ready for meditation? Fasten your seat belts. Let's fly!' He clearly wasn't wasting any time. The short but deep meditation felt very refreshing.

The moderator asked Gurudev to share his experience on a contemporary hotspot. After all, one could spin the globe and stop it anywhere, and one is likely to be within an inch or two of a conflict. I was almost certain that Gurudev would share his adventures from Iraq—especially the one where he went into a designated red zone without any accompanying security, to meet with Shia leaders. When he was advised against crossing the green zone, he had assured everyone that he had his own security. And then he had set out by himself.

Or maybe he'd talk about his attempt to reach out to ISIS, who sent him gory beheaded images in return, suggesting that would be his fate if he were to go visit them.

'I have one failure story and one success story,' Gurudev responded after pausing for a few seconds. His face turned pensive—as if he were replaying the series of events in his mind.

A failure story? My antennae went up. I didn't think a Guru could fail!

It was September 2006. The president of Sri Lanka had promised the role of deputy prime minister to Velupillai Prabhakaran, the chief of the militant separatist group called LTTE, should he decide to give up arms and end the conflict.

With the president's assurance, Gurudev had gone to speak to Prabhakaran. It was tough. The army had dropped him off at one location, and from there he had to walk through a piece of land that was full of landmines to get to the militants' area. It was a stretch of no man's land where no one dared to flutter during those months of conflict. In my mind, I imagined a scene straight out of a James Bond movie.

Gurudev urged Prabhakaran to drop his weapons, but that didn't work. The militant chief was overconfident about their military prowess.

'But his subordinates had tears in their eyes. They said we wish our leader accepted your proposal.' He didn't. The bloody war continued.

After much bloodshed and a tremendous loss of lives, Prabhakaran's lieutenant eventually called Gurudev.

They were ready to surrender, and they requested that Gurudev mediate with the government.

Gurudev convinced the president to agree on a peaceful settlement. The president asked Gurudev to relay that the militants could come in with a white flag, and that they shall be given amnesty.

'It was the most . . .' Gurudev struggled to find the right word. '. . . ghastly thing that could have ever happened.' His tone softened as he recalled the most painful experience of his life.

Gurudev conveyed the message to the LTTE, and based on his word, they went with the white flag. As soon as they came close, the army opened fire at point-blank range. Thousands were massacred that day.

When he tried to reach out to the president, he was told that the president's orders somehow hadn't reached the troops on the ground.

I could sense the pain and helplessness in Gurudev's tone as he recalled this bait and switch.

Despite all this, the Art of Living's volunteers had jumped in for trauma relief efforts. SKY breath and meditation were taught to a stadium full of captives, in order to help them release the painful trauma of this violent episode.

'This was very sad.' He moved on. 'But a success story was in Colombia.'

Finally! I had always wanted to hear this story. Gurudev's mediation efforts in Colombia had played out just a couple of years ago. Since then, I had done quite a bit of research about the mediation. I had spoken to local journalists. I had also developed a rapport with Francisco, who was instrumental in facilitating the FARC intervention. My memory flashed back to my meeting last year with Francisco, a tall young man with wavy hair, a lanky build, and dogged determination. Fran, as everyone called him, had shared his FARC story with me. This was the very first time I was going to hear the entire account from Gurudev directly.

The government of Colombia and FARC—a guerrilla movement—have been involved in a gruelling armed conflict since the sixties. The atrocities committed by FARC over time have killed over 20,00,000 people and rendered nearly 70,00,000 homeless. Pablo Escobar and all the graphic depictions in 'Narcos' pale in comparison to the destruction during the FARC conflict.

Fran, along with several local Art of Living volunteers from Colombia had come to see Gurudev at the Canadian ashram. The locals were asking Gurudev to do something about the longest, most bloody civil war between the FARC and the government of Colombia. At the time, the peace process was already in its third year, but it distinctly lacked clarity.

The passion in Fran's voice was hard to ignore, and so was his uvular pronunciation of the letter 'R' in FARC as he tried to explain to me how convoluted the conflict had eventually become.

President Andres Pastrana was the first hopeful president who initiated the peace process. However, FARC didn't show up at the ceremony, leaving an empty chair, or *La Silla Vacia*—which then became a symbol of a failed peace process. I remembered protesting and boycotting university exams during my undergraduate degree— leaving an empty chair. The consequences I had to face were not remotely close.

'These guerrilla soldiers are suffering from insomnia, anxiety and trauma due to the conditions of the Colombian jungle and the unending war.' Gurudev said this even before the Colombian volunteers had completed their story.

He then looked at Fran and asked him to contact FARC leaders to let them know that the Art of Living Foundation could support the peace process. And that was that. Fran began to laugh, recalling this wild goose chase. Guerrilla leaders who had been hiding in the jungle didn't really have a 'Contact Us' page on a website. Nor did they have any interest in interacting with outsiders.

As fate would have it, around that time, Colombia honoured Gurudev by conferring the highest civilian award upon him for his work in Colombia spanning over a decade.

'I had a ceremonial five-minute-long handshake meeting with President Santos, which lasted over fifty minutes.' Gurudev began narrating the second story.

Just a month before that, Gurudev had asked Fran to go to Havana, Cuba, and meet with FARC leaders. 'You will meet many people. Talk to all of them.' Gurudev instructed him.

Fran was perplexed. He knew no one. He flew down to Havana anyway, and to his surprise, one inquiry led to another and within two days he landed a meeting with FARC.

Gurudev continued, 'The president looked a little worried that the peace process was not going anywhere. I told him, why don't I go there and give it a try.' President Santos accepted Gurudev's offer of help.

He went to Havana to meet with the FARC. Initially, they refused to talk to him. They said they were Marxist and had nothing to do with a guru. 'We stay at arm's length from spiritual people.' Gurudev chuckled as he recalled FARC's first response.

Gurudev spoke at the University of Havana that evening. Some of the FARC representatives were in the audience. They had come to investigate who this person really was.

'Next day, fifteen of their commandoes came to see me.'
The talks began.

Gurudev emphasized that he understood them completely and was fully in support of their fight for justice. 'You're not having fun in the forest with your guns. I understand you. You are dedicating your life for social justice, for that I am with you. The entire world is with you.'

The FARC leaders probably guessed that there was a 'But' coming soon, but they didn't anticipate what would follow that.

'But only if you adopt non-violent means.'

Gurudev made that very clear. He reminded them that fifty years had passed, and the violence had not taken them anywhere.

As an example, Gurudev talked about the Naxalites of eastern India who had similar ideologies, and about how they met a violent end. He asked them thought-provoking questions and drew parallels from his experience with similar situations. At the same time, he was also giving them lessons in non-violence and sharing spiritual wisdom. He was carefully navigating through various emotions—appealing to logic, touching hearts and gaining trust with his words.

A senior commander lost his patience at that point. He didn't seem to think any of this would work, and so he tried to do what people usually do when they have to make difficult decisions. Buy time. He tried to convince everyone that they should stop all this and go back to what they had been doing. This interjection created an awkward silence in the room.

A silence that Gurudev broke.

'Time will eat the fruit of your actions.' He said. 'You do it else time will.'

The FARC leaders protested that they couldn't accept Gandhian principles of non-violence. They had lost so many of their soldiers. How would they face their families? Gurudev recalls how FARC thought that adopting non-violence would be considered hypocritical and a complete U-turn from their fifty-year-old ideologies.

'I said, "Okay, never mind. Let's meditate!"' Gurudev said, bringing his palms to his lap and momentarily closing his eyes in an affable gesture. Gaston Hall was amused. Perhaps the vivid imagery of weapon-bearing, hard-core guerrilla commanders sitting around a guru and meditating had just crossed everyone's minds.

Fran, who was acting as a translator all this time, almost fell off his chair. Really? Would FARC guerrillas close their eyes and meditate?

But they did. All of them. And they loved it.

This routine continued for three days. The FARC would bring up all the different reasons why they couldn't drop their arms. Gurudev would patiently listen, offer his point of view, and towards the end, they all would meditate together.

'At the end of the third day, they all came with me to the press conference where FARC said, "We accept the Gandhian principles of non-violence and have declared a unilateral cease-fire."' Gurudev said with a triumphant expression on his face.

The crowd erupted in applause.

Towards the end, they were all addressing him as Master. My journey from knowing him as Sri Sri to recognizing him as Gurudev could fill a book. Meanwhile, it had taken these people only a few hours. Who was more evolved? I wondered.

One of the commanders came to him and said, 'I have only seen wooden and stone figures of saints before, but today I stand before a living saint.' He then handed Gurudev two stones—one to be returned so that their people may touch the stone and feel his presence.

I thought about how effortless and unassuming he made it all appear. Five decades of war, millions killed and displaced, and all it took was three days of talking and meditations to reverse the course of history. They didn't even speak the same language. They held guns. He wore a white robe.

Fran's work wasn't done just yet. Later, he went to Cuba and taught Sudarshan Kriya to thousands of FARC members. 'We couldn't find a big enough space so we'd do it in cinema halls during the day.' Fran had never spoken in front of such big audiences before. 'I felt like a rock star,' he laughed. He deserved it.

FARC didn't stop at dropping arms or learning SKY and meditation. In the months that followed, they asked Fran to arrange a meeting between FARC and the families of civilians killed at their hands. In these meetings, FARC extended an olive branch and asked for forgiveness. The perpetrators and affected families held hands and hugged. Tears of forgiveness washed away the bitterness.

Later on, with the help of a reporter, I would get an opportunity to speak to Ivan Marques, one of the senior FARC leaders. The phone connection was too weak for us to cross the language barrier. But he sounded thankful to Gurudev. And he promised to send a video message.

As the talk ended, I quietly left the hall, ruminating over what Gurudev had said. I had no desire to stay back and socialize with some acquaintances I had run into earlier.

I couldn't stop thinking about these so-called terrorists in Colombia. How they too melted when they experienced unconditional acceptance. Gurudev had solved the conflict through compassion, grace, and love.

I stopped and closed my eyes as I walked past the gardens on O Street. I felt ignorant to be holding on to emotional baggage from my personal battle with terrorism. It was not worth it. Fortunately, I didn't require a stone as a reminder. I had Gurudev.

'Behind every culprit, there is a victim crying for help. You heal the victim, and the culprit goes away.' Gurudev's words were settling in.

I imagined the culprit closing the door behind him.

Soliloquy on Death

It was the thirteenth anniversary of 9/11. I was walking the grounds of the World Trade Center Memorial. I was there to pay my respects and express my gratitude. The entire area, dotted by hundreds of white oaks, is now quite a meditative and contemplative space. I walked to the footprint of the towers. Where majestic structures once stood are now giant waterfalls and reflection pools. They reflect a strange sense of absence. Even light is unable to escape this man-made void, lined with tall, pitch-black granite walls.

The names of those who perished are inscribed in thick bronze plates installed along the perimeters of the pools. Hundreds of candles and flowers adorned these names that day. That wasn't always the case. I tried to keep my eyes away from it, but for some reason I couldn't. It read like a dense, macabre poem.

Death is such an equalizer. An absolute certainty of life. As a matter of fact, everything else is plainly uncertain.

I began to wonder how one of the very few things in life that is not subjective is also so elusive.

Usually, there is a concept in the mind and a corresponding image. For example, think of a banana and a yellow fruit pops up. But death? No visualization helps. Just a sense of 'there's-no-one-home' and a feeling of fear or grief. Nothing even comes close. Can death be known at all? I don't know. But one thing I know is that ignoring the notion of it or pushing it away simply creates a false sense of permanence.

A thin sheet of water continuously poured down from all four sides of the pool and disappeared into a bottomless pit. There was some grandeur it was trying to convey, but I failed to decrypt it. The sound of the cascades successfully muted the otherwise noisy city.

One evening in Canada, I asked Gurudev about death. I imagined that one who knows so much about life and living must know what lies beyond. He shared an innocent story from his childhood.

As a young child, Ravi was very curious. He would always accompany his parents to places of worship. And whenever he saw a ceremony being performed in any temple or spiritual setting, he would keenly observe it and then imitate it once alone at home.

One day a priest came to hear about this, and he instructed Gurudev's family not to let him see the Śrāddha ceremony. In the Hindu tradition, this ceremony is performed to pay homage to one's deceased ancestors.

Taking the advice of this wise man, every time the ritual was performed, Ravi was strictly forbidden from being near it. The ritual could go on for hours, and he would have to remain confined in a room. This would get very difficult for the curious six year old. He would peek through the cracks in the wooden door and unsuccessfully try to make sense of whatever was going on.

One day, an elderly gentleman in his neighbourhood passed away. Young Ravi was quarantined away in his room so that he would not see the last rites and related ceremonies. Once his mother had locked the room and left, he climbed up the ledge of the window and in a rather uncomfortable posture, watched the entire ceremony through a small opening in the windowpane.

In those days, there was a lake across from Gurudev's home. The family of the deceased carried the dead body to the lake, placed it on a funeral pyre, and cremated the body. The pyre burned all through the night. The glowing embers from the fire rose high up into the dark sky. Ravi looked at it from the ledge of the window. At some point, in a state of exhaustion, he fell asleep by the window for a few hours. He woke up just before dawn broke and found the fire still burning, albeit with much less intensity. Out of curiosity, Ravi wanted to venture near the pyre, but getting past his aunt and grandmother was challenging.

Though he ended up not going to the lake, looking at death from such proximity had engulfed Ravi in feelings of curiosity and familiarity. Time would eventually unfold its mysteries to him. Watching the burning pyre through most of the night had been a surreal experience.

'As I stood gazing at the rising fire, strangely enough, it all appeared intimately familiar, he said.

A little girl walked forward and lay a rose bud on one of the names on the bronze plate. In that emotional moment, I couldn't help but wonder how at one level, death is so familiar, and yet at another level it is completely unrecognizable. Just the thought of death creates a vacuum.

Indeed, it was this void that served as a wakeup call for me and was one of the main triggers that led me to the spiritual path. It was from this void that the quest to discover the purpose of my life emerged.

NDE or Near Death Experiences are not new. In the book, *Proof of Heaven*, a neurosurgeon describes his journey into the afterlife and back. A chill ran down my spine as I learned how Dr Alexander's brain, gripped by a rare form of bacterial meningitis, went from an almost vegetative state to a full awakening. When he woke up, he was a changed man, certain of a life that lies beyond death.

Not everyone is lucky enough to make a comeback from the edge of a cliff. So how does one get to experience what happens after death?

'You will see the body out there. Just like a discarded, worn piece of garment. Once you come out of the body, you will see your whole life flashing like a movie in a few minutes.' Gurudev explained what happens after death as if he was explaining to a lost tourist what lay after the blind turn ahead.

'. . . and in that final moment, only two things will matter. How much love you gave and how much knowledge you received.'

Was that the overarching purpose of this journey of life? Give love and gain knowledge. I repeated this in my head several times.

Constant awareness of the impermanence of everything is sufficient to not let one get stuck in the grind of daily life. But at the same time, the paranoia could simply wipe out the charm of living.

In some sense, death ought to be liberating. The first of the Four Noble Truths in Buddhism states that all life is suffering. If that is indeed the case, then surely the culmination of it calls for celebration. It must feel good to get past all of life's drama. I guess that's why so many traditions honour death. The Catholic All Souls' Day is a colourful celebration of the dead. The Buddhist festival of Bon in Japan signifies the same. Hindus observe Pitru Paksha. And so on.

As I glanced towards the western sky, painted in hues of saffron and pink, I felt grateful to have this knowledge.

We are energy, and the laws of physics say that energy cannot be destroyed, which means that birth and death can't be the bookends of this life. Looking at the continuous flow of water in the eternity pool by the memorial, I couldn't help but wonder if indeed there was a beginning and an end to life as we know it.

The water in the pool reflected the sense of tranquillity and sombreness that I felt inside, and that was oddly comforting.

'Onipa'a

It was a clear starry night. There was a strange calmness in the atmosphere. The silence of the night was broken again and again by the uninterrupted lashing of waves on Waikiki beach. The salty breeze from the ocean mixed with the fragrance of Tuberose and Plumeria flowers of the intricately woven Lei swathed the entire room in a strange intoxication. Far in the distance, lights from thousands of homes on the face of the hill created the illusion of an illuminated tapestry covering the land.

That summer, I had seized an opportunity to travel with Gurudev to Hawaii. We had just returned to the hotel after attending his talk at the Hawaii Theatre in Honolulu.

It was already well past my bedtime, but I was not complaining. The thrill of spending time with Gurudev far outweighed other distractions such as sleep. 'It appears that those lights are trying to fight with the night to dispel the darkness. From another perspective, the same situation appears as if the dark night is giving these tiny lights an opportunity to express themselves,' Gurudev spoke after a brief period of silence.

His eyes were on the distant horizon. My eyes were on him.

Was he referring to the faculty of perception? 'Illusion is an error in perception . . .' His words from the Waldorf Astoria were clearly etched in my memory, even after thirteen years.

'Irrespective of the situation, it is how one perceives it that creates the foundation for their actions.' He added.

Bangalore, India's tech capital today, was struck with an epidemic of the plague in the early 1900s. There was chaos on the streets, and many neighbourhoods were evacuated. Those left behind were rendered ghastly. People abandoned their homes en masse. Amidst this mayhem, there was one woman who stayed behind with her three children.

This woman was Gurudev's grandmother. 'A beautiful lady with a bright round face, long hair, a beaming smile and a persona of brilliance.' Bhanu, Gurudev's younger sister would proudly reminisce.

Athey-Amma, as Gurudev would affectionately call her, was a kind and gentle woman. He would fondly remember her as someone who inspired not just her family, but everyone around her, to be resilient and to live in the moment. Her life had not turned out to be an easy one. But her innate courage and humour shone through the unfavourable situations.

I felt sleepy after a long day of travel, but Gurudev had just begun to share some glimpses of his family tree, and I didn't want to miss it.

The challenges that life brought Athey-Amma had never repressed her free spirit. Her deep-rooted faith and courage became somewhat of a legacy that was passed on to the next generations.

Gurudev's grandfather lived an ascetic life in service of the nation. After nearly a century and a half of oppression, India had awakened and reclaimed its independence from the British Raj. Mahatma Gandhi had inspired millions to join his non-violent civil disobedience movement. Gurudev's grandfather was one of them.

Gurudev's father would reminisce over an incident when Mahatma Gandhi visited Bangalore at the helm of the freedom movement. Gurudev's grandfather collected all the gold from their home, including his wife's jewellery, much of which was a family heirloom, and offered it all to Mahatma Gandhi's freedom movement. The only jewellery Athey-Amma retained was one thin ceremonial gold chain and another small piece of jewellery gifted by her brother. In the blink of an eye, he gave away nearly twenty-three pounds of gold—the only source of savings they had at the time.

Gandhiji accepted the gracious charity. He then looked at Gurudev's father, an eight-year-old boy then. Gandhi gestured and drew him closer.

'Is that really required?' he said, pointing at a gold chain around the child's neck. Without thinking twice, Gurudev's grandfather immediately removed it and offered that to Gandhiji as well.

Gurudev's grandfather spent several years of his life in service to India, along with Mahatma Gandhi, in the Sabarmati Ashram in Gujarat. He was a simple and passionate individual who had pledged his entire life to the country's freedom movement. Little did he know that someday his grandson was to start a freedom movement of his own—freeing society from stress and violence.

I couldn't help myself from reflecting on how there were moments in life when I felt so stuck—as if I had no freedom. Who is stuck and who is seeking freedom? Isn't the one seeking freedom already free?

Athey-Amma gave birth to ten children. Only three survived into adulthood; Gurudev's father, his younger brother, and his sister. Pitaji, as he was addressed, was the eldest. He was barely seventeen when his father passed away, right after returning from the country's freedom movement. His passing was a blow to the family. Often, when the patriarch of a tightly knit family passes away, it throws the surviving family into disarray. This time, it was no different.

Suddenly, the family fortune dwindled to rock bottom. Everything changed overnight for a family that had once been respected as Diwans (administrators) of the time. They lived hand-to-mouth, as each evening Athey-Amma struggled to put food on the table.

Adversity affects people differently. Some lose faith, become hopeless and drown themselves in self-pity. Then there are some like Athey-Amma, who can hold the family together with ties of love and humour during a rather trying phase of life.

This was the foundation upon which young Gurudev's value system was built.

My eyes admired the luminance of the hill in the distance and my mind was at ease, reflecting on some of the events from my past. Just like a dark night provides an opportunity for lights to shine, adversity evokes abilities which, in normal circumstances, would have lain dormant.

I momentarily flashed back to my Gandhian school days. A strict and modest atmosphere with limited means. Wearing handspun white *khadi* uniforms that effortlessly added layers of dorkiness. Studying in Gujarati, the regional dialect. The strict Gandhian ambience did not fit my definition of cool in any imaginable way. At that time,

I was envious of other kids in more progressive schools, studying in English and flaunting modern attire. I felt so imperfect and deficient back then. But looking back, I feel ever so fortunate to have had that kind of grounding and simple life experiences, especially during those formative years. There was a thin slice of Gurudev's value system that I could personally identify with.

It was getting late. The waves continued to lash against the shore. The room was still fragrant. Gurudev smiled and gestured that the party had come to an end.

The volcanic tuff cone of Diamond Head crater was standing tall and firm in the backdrop, softly whispering "Onipa'a . . . 'Onipa'a . . . 'Onipa'a . . . Be steadfast in the face of adversity.'

V

Homecoming

Truth be told, coming back home never gets old.

Wheel within a Wheel

Beyond an event is knowledge.
Beyond a person is love.
Beyond an object is infinity.

—Gurudev

I was at the Art of Living Retreat Centre in North Carolina for a week-long retreat with Gurudev. At that particular moment, I was on my way to his kutir. I had my laptop with me, as I was excited to share a piece I had written for this book with Gurudev.

He was ready to call it a night. There were three of us in the room. We were the last ones standing.

'Hmmm? So, what have you been writing lately?' A very familiar question greeted me. This time, I was a bit more prepared but equally self-conscious. 'I've written about that evening in Berlin, where you chipped away my writer's block.' I then gently asked if he would be interested if I read it to him. He nodded with a smile.

I started reading. 'This one is titled, "The unexpected demise of writer's block."'

The activities of a full day have come to an end. The hallways of the usually buzzing Maritime Hotel are quiet. Outside, the wind is blowing hard. Alpine peaks have collected quite a bit of snow today and so tomorrow morning Berlin will wake up to a fine dusting.

'Wait, did you mean Berlin will get snow because of proximity to Alps?' He laughed heartily.

Dinner was served. I was ready to eat crow. I attempted to explain what I really meant there, but I couldn't find suitable words. I tried to save face, but I could come up with nothing to substantiate my claim.

'My dear, the entire Germany lies between those two!'

I was nervous. This hadn't started as well as I had expected. But I continued bravely.

On most occasions, my mind would be calm and settled; reflecting on events from throughout the day. Tonight, it's a different story.

Gurudev is just finishing his dinner in the adjacent alcove of the suite, which has been turned into a quiet dining space for one. I am sitting in the dimly lit living room. Unlike the frigid air outside, the temperature inside is just right. The faint fragrance of jasmine is silently making its way to the farthest corner of the room.

'Wait, wait. Are you sure there were jasmines in the room? Because you don't get them in Germany.' Gurudev lifted his head from what he was reading and pulled the rug from under my creative prose. I closed my eyes and tried to recall the fragrance in the room. I couldn't recall anything anymore.

'I don't recall, Gurudev. I'll just remove this reference.' I was already waving my white flag.

By now, the people in the room were having a jolly good time at my expense. They were enjoying the sight of me simmering in the thick soup of my own making. One of them kept silently pointing out the window and asked me if I could see the Alps from here too. Others were laughing in a way Gurudev didn't notice. With the fortitude of a warrior, I continued.

As I look around the hotel room, I silently concede that it is a bit too ornate for my choice but quite appropriately appointed for a classic European hotel. The wallpaper in the room carries subtle, yet intricate art work and a matte sheen. A small glass chandelier is reflecting through elaborate mirrors in the hallway, lending additional expanse to the room. The furniture has been rearranged in the room so that it can accommodate many and yet not look overly crowded. The floor is lined with crisp white sheets immaculately stretched from wall to wall.

'Too long a description. Instead, you should write about any wisdom you derived from that scene. A wise one finds wisdom in everything around him. And did the room really have wallpaper?'

The people in the room had now dropped everything they were doing so that they could enjoy the roast of a struggling writer. I assured him that I didn't make up anything, including the part about the wallpaper, and continued reading.

On the surface, this building is like any other hotel. However, this very space is just a few blocks away from the remains of the Berlin Wall, a structure that once physically and ideologically separated humanity. Now this location is hosting over a thousand people from all over the world for a week-long meditation workshop. What a difference time and circumstances make.

No comments. What a relief. I continued reading.

Gurudev walks into the room. My immediate reflex is to stand up. He acknowledges it back with a smile and signals me to be at ease and sit. I use the opportunity to move a little closer to his seat. There is a stack of letters and paperwork waiting to be attended to. Instead, he picks up a greeting card displayed on the table next to his couch. He opens it and smiles. I crane my neck to see what's in it. Noticing my effort, he passes over the card to me without saying a word.

Inside is a crayon drawing of a green and blue ball. The image, resembling the earth, have stick figures of a bearded man and a little girl holding hands and standing on the globe. 'Lisa heart Gurudev' reads the card. I couldn't really tell whether it was the innocence or the creativity of the little one that touched my heart.

'So, what have you been writing lately?' Gurudev breaks the silence.

Not too long ago the same question had been asked. This moment felt like textbook déjà vu. I kept going.

Gurudev knows that I like to write about various topics and has made it a point to ask me about my latest musings each time we meet. I have been expecting this question since the first day I landed in Germany, yet am as unprepared as ever with a clear answer.

'Umm . . . a few things Gurudev. I'm writing about how I accidently stumbled upon Art of Living and how my life changed after that. I want to compile my experiences with and around you in the form of a book.'

I tell him about my grand plans while realizing that like a nervous teenager, I'm using the words 'umm' and 'like' as unnecessary fillers. The room is silent. A few other people in the room appear to be minding their own business. More realistically, their ears are finely tuned to capture every word of the exchange.

The silence is killing me. I then let it out.

'I feel a bit stuck though. This writer's block is for real. And funny thing is that I'm not even a professional writer. Sometimes I wonder who will even read what I write! What will people think if I come up with something mediocre?' My pedestrian fears pop out.

As I read this line, I reflected on how far I had come since then.

There. I said it. The immediate relief I feel at having gotten this load off my chest is instantaneously replaced by embarrassment. I was feeling stupid to have blurted out something so silly.

He simply smiled and didn't say anything. He was looking outside the French windows from the tenth floor of the hotel room. I wondered what he was looking at. There is not much of a view in the dark of the night apart from a very long and empty road. The road has become completely silent and wet due to the flurries that have melted immediately upon hitting the ground. There is no accumulation just yet. The wet jet-black road is dramatically reflecting an array of traffic lights hanging from above at precise intervals.

The stillness on the road outside was competing with silence inside the room.

'Look at these traffic lights,' he said.

The hues of the lights were painting the surface of the road in one color before changing to another. We stand there observing the traffic lights for several minutes. I'm wondering what he will say next. Clearly so far, I wasn't seeing what he was.

Back in Boone, Gurudev was standing by the window looking at the moon outside. I continued to read further.

'Look at these lights. They keep going on, oblivious to the fact that there are no cars on the road. It is exactly following the laws of nature.'

I wasn't sure where he was going with this.

'The flowers bloom in the forest whether someone is looking at them or not. The birds sing whether someone values their perfectly attuned melodies or not. Clouds change their colors. Rainbows appear. Do they wait for someone to appreciate them? Nature displays its beauty whether there is a beholder or not.'

I paused to see if he wanted to say something. Silence. I felt relief as strains of confidence began to emerge. For a change, the others in the room had turned pensive.

I am amazed at how despite having looked at hundreds, if not thousands of traffic lights over the course of my lifetime, I have never really seen them. The rhythmic movement of these changing lights in the stillness of the night have so much wisdom to offer.

We stand there watching.

The traffic lights continue their dance. Red, yellow, green, yellow . . .

'It was a still night and the distant grey clouds offered an intermittent glimpse of the stars beyond them.' Gurudev offered some finishing touches while reminiscing about that evening. He then walked out of the room silently.

'Hey man, enlighten us if you see Alps outside these windows too.' So much for the pensive environment. A smart aleck didn't miss the opportunity to pull my leg as soon we were alone. The others burst into laughter. With a lot of effort, I kept smiling.

My ego appeared to be mortally wounded. Why did Gurudev have me expose my writing in front of everyone?

How fickle the mind is. At one level, I felt so much joy in sharing my writing with the one whose approval mattered the most. Yet at another level, just a little sarcasm from my friends in the room had ruffled my feathers. We seem to exist in a field charged with contradictions and opposites.

A version of me from ten years ago would have been caught up in this storm of emotions. That day, I was much more aware of what was brewing around me. And just that awareness alone had dropped me into the eye of the storm, where it is always quiet. A silence that is surrounded by disturbance. I was a silent, and perhaps slightly disturbed, witness to my thoughts.

Enlightenment Is For . . .

Just like there is rice inside the paddy, knowledge is there within. You just need to lose the husk . . .

—Gurudev

The other day in Boone, while walking up and down the slopes of the Art of Living Retreat Centre, I got into an intense conversation with Banka. He called me a loser. And towards the end of our talk, I realized that over the last fifteen years or so of walking the path laid out by Gurudev, I really hadn't gained anything.

I over-meditated. It is just like oversleeping, except it usually feels good. But not that day. I was feeling horrible that I wouldn't be able to make it in time to see Gurudev. It was a chilly December morning in Boone. I rushed out of my room in Zambezi—one of the many buildings in the retreat centre—and dashed towards Gurudev's kutir.

Alak would have already arrived, and I was sure to find Banka there as well. I negotiated the first uphill slope with the dexterity of a sprinter, but soon I was slowed down by the combination of a mean second hill and the multitude of 'Jai Gurudevs' that I had to exchange with the scores of people walking in the other direction. More laughing, happy people walking away from the kutir simply meant that Gurudev was probably done meeting everyone and had gone upstairs to meditate. I was not giving up. I picked up the pace.

I made it in. Just a few people were left in the meeting space on the first floor. Gurudev was walking towards the staircase leading up to his room. He saw me dashing in like a tornado. He had a mischievous smile on his face. I wondered what he was up to.

'Haan Kushal!'

Swoooshhh . . . That's the sound of someone emptying a large bucket of honey over me. That's how it feels when he calls me by my name. He hadn't said anything yet and I felt so at home in that moment. Om sweet Om.

'You're late. You missed something important,' Gurudev teased me.

'What did I miss, Gurudev?' I asked helplessly, still dripping with imaginary honey.

'Enlightenment.' He blinked his eyes with a broad grin on his face.

'Who cares about enlightenment, Gurudev . . . I have you!'

I couldn't believe I just said that. Words arose spontaneously and then spilled all over, poking me on their way out. I froze for a moment. Am I the same person who, once upon a time, resisted letting this larger-than-life phenomenon into my life?

Gurudev laughed. The lightness and warmth in his presence diffused the heartbeat in my throat. He paused and then walked back to his couch. He picked up a little plastic bottle and placed a couple of drops of 'enlightenment liquid' on my fingers.

Enlightenment was but a concept in my mind until I spent more time with Gurudev. For the longest time, I struggled to understand it, let alone be able to explain it. I still haven't understood it fully. Asking him about it was not of much use.

'Those who know will never tell,' Gurudev always says.

On a warm summer evening by Boston Harbour, I found myself in a hotel room with Gurudev. The suite had a little annex space attached to it, where all the food was kept for Gurudev and a few people travelling with him. The living room had turned into a meeting space full of people. And a lot more people were waiting outside the room to meet him. It was getting closer to dinner time, and over a hundred people had still not met him. He got up and walked to the annex. I followed him there. The room was small. Two women who had prepared the food were waiting patiently so that they could serve food for Gurudev. They too were surprised to see him in that room. Like a health inspector in a kitchen, he started checking the food simmering under warm aluminium foils. He signalled for me to pass him a couple of empty food trays and, like an alchemist, started mixing up food with rice in those party platter trays.

'Call everyone. They must be hungry.' He asked another person in the room. One of the ladies whispered to me with a tense expression on her face. There just wasn't enough food for so many of us. But before I could even think about that, people were lining up and Gurudev was ready with a ladle in his hands to serve food.

Anybody who has spent some time around Gurudev has what they call a 'Guru Story' or two to tell. A little happening that defies logic. A little dip in the ocean of all possibilities. Something that seems so improbable, yet it happens in a very casual fashion.

He began serving food to everyone, one by one. Word spread fast that the master was serving food. More and more people showed up. He kept serving them with a smile. One after another. That evening Gurudev stood in the little annex space for almost two hours, patiently meeting with and serving food to nearly 500 people. Neither the women who cooked for just thirty people, nor I have, to this day, figured out how on the earth that amount of food fed hundreds of people on that warm summer evening by Boston Harbour.

What if we were living in a giant simulation? And perhaps enlightenment is simply gaining the ability to be able to simulate any experience for anyone, anywhere.

There are innumerable such Guru stories I have personally come across. People being mysteriously healed to the complete disbelief of their doctors, people having their smallest of desires fulfilled, people navigating their way out when they are completely lost—literally and metaphorically. The list goes on.

Once, I happened to be with Gurudev in King of Prussia, Pennsylvania, where a lady with severe arthritic leg pain had come to see him. She could barely walk without the support of her husband. Although she was in so much pain, she had somehow managed to come see Gurudev.

'Jump.' That's all he said when she spoke to him. I was perplexed. And so was she. He repeated the same instructions. And the lady got up and leapt up in the air like a little girl. She had tears in her eyes, and she was so disoriented, that when she walked out of the room, she left her walking cane behind.

There are some questions that have no answers. How does Gurudev impact so many people? How does one go to him and instantly feel connected? How does everyone feel like they have a one-on-one relationship with him? How does everyone feel so loved and cared for when they are around him? Why do questions disappear in his presence? How does the mind become inexplicably thoughtless around him? How did he come up with Sudarshan Kriya, which has impacted millions around the planet? How can someone be so unconditionally giving all the time? One really can't fake this stuff.

There are some questions that have no answers. And perhaps such questions have but one explanation.

I was not quite sure what I was supposed to do with the enlightenment liquid between my fingers. Gurudev asked me to bring it to my nose and take a really deep breath. I followed the instructions to my own peril as my brain almost exploded. It was like someone had shot wasabi bullets up my nostrils. I blacked out for a second, but regained consciousness in the next moment, only to find everyone around me laughing at my animated reaction. My eyes began to water uncontrollably. I felt a bout of freshness as all the fatigue in my system seemed to have dripped out along with the tears. It was an Ayurvedic herb that opened up all the energy channels in the head. If that is all there is to enlightenment, then I certainly don't care about it.

Gurudev says enlightenment is a joke. It's like a fish going in search of water. It is all about going back to one's very own innocent nature, despite the intelligence. It's a journey from words to silence. From head to heart.

A master had two disciples. One was an elderly man who had been ardently meditating for many hours a day for over twenty years. He once asked the master how long it would take for him to be enlightened. When the master responded that it would take him three lifetimes, he was furious and frustrated. He threw away his rosary and left. The second disciple was a young boy. The master told him it would take him as many lifetimes as the leaves on the tree they were sitting under. Hearing this, the boy started dancing. Only that many leaves! At least they are countable. It is said that in that very moment the boy achieved enlightenment.

Like my pen moving at a relaxed pace on the paper, I kept ambling down this path, with little idea of what the destination looked like or how far it was.

So then why was I so upset at Banka for calling me a loser?

He was once again right. Along the path, I had lost a lot of stress and many deep-rooted impressions.

I had lost a piece of my conditioned mind. The tendency to doubt everything, wanting to find the hidden muffin.

I had lost the tendency to be swayed by others' opinions or judgements. Many of my fears as well. I could take risks.

And even if I fail, I know I will never be alone. There is an invisible safety net somewhere. I know it.

I had lost the ability and willingness to distinguish between all-knowing and not-knowing. And some day, I hope I will lose my remaining ignorance. I hope that I will have nothing left to hold on to. And in that nothingness, maybe I'll find something that is everything. Perhaps, one day, 'I am that everything' will no longer be a concept, but an irrefutable experience.

When Buddha became enlightened, someone asked the awakened one what he gained. He responded with a content smile, saying that he didn't gain anything, he just lost everything.

I have been a sore loser over the last fifteen years. And I still have so much more to lose. Enlightenment is, after all, for losers.

The Visitor Who Never Left

As the sun set over the Hudson, I closed my eyes to meditate in an attempt to hit the reset button on an otherwise long and stressful day. The simple act of closing my eyes consciously enveloped me in darkness, drawing me inwards. A storm of thoughts arose as visual distractions subsided. Amidst the scores of thoughts, the loudest appeared to be the most existential one—what was I going to have for dinner that night? More thoughts came and left, but this one hung around like a pinned post on my Facebook newsfeed. I wanted to enjoy my signature rasam ramen noodles that day, but I felt a complete lack of willingness to cook. Perhaps I could just order in some curry. I couldn't seem to decide what was more annoying—the trivial nature of the thought itself, or its dogged persistence. It was clear that it didn't want to leave me alone.

I invoked the three golden rules for meditation as prescribed by Gurudev. I do nothing. I want nothing.

I am nothing. Relax. No effort is required, I told myself. Just repose. It helped marginally. It was time to bring in the big guns. I took a deep breath and brought my Sahaj mantra into my mind. Like a Jedi wielding a light sabre, I observed all my thoughts collapse lifelessly on the sticky surface of my mind like loose garments. There was absolute quiet. I felt like I had been transported from walking around in a noisy marketplace to a coal mine thousands of feet underneath the earth. It was pitch dark and silent. I could almost hear myself breathe. The silence was thick yet delicate, cloistral yet alive. Nourishing and healing. I felt a little flutter in the space between my eyebrows.

Knock. Knock. Knock.

A sequence of loud knocks catapulted me out of this dreamy state. There you go. I was back on the surface again, falling towards a fast-approaching cloud of thoughts.

'Whoever it is, please just get lost.' I wished silently and refused to answer. 'There is no one in here.' I again asked in my mind.

A few moments passed by, and I was beginning to feel relieved that the considerate intruder had heard my silent prayer to leave me be.

Knock. Knock.

'Who is it?' This time I asked without moving. The room fell silent again.

'It's me.' The uninvited guest whispered. 'I'm here to talk to you.' My antennae perked up.

'Who's "me"?' I am still struggling with the answer.

'You have felt my presence even before you really met me.'

'That's poetic but quickly make your point. I want to go back to my meditation.'

'Not everything I tell you is pleasant or comprehensible on the first go. But you have always been better off listening to me.'

'Even my wife could say the same thing but go on. I'm listening.'

'I am the one who asked you to leave the burning towers on the day everything changed. I am the one who silently pushed you to go to the Waldorf Astoria on the day when everything changed for you yet again.'

I smiled now that the intruder's identity was confirmed.

'You saw me clearly after your first experience of meditation. And since then, you have followed me unknowingly like a musk deer chases the whiff of his own fragrance.'

'You came looking for me either when you felt completely lost, curious or uncertain. And I came looking for you when you felt complete. When you were "home". Often after your meditations or during long walks in nature.'

Before I could relive those moments, he continued.

'I am not ashamed to admit that encouraging you to learn to meditate was completely self-serving in a way. For only in those moments you could hear me loud and clear.'

'I'm responsible for a lot of firsts in your life. It was me who told you Alak was the one when you saw her for the first time. I almost twisted your arm to take the red pill and go down this path of the Self. I helped you skilfully manoeuvre and move past your own discomfort of the first satsang, and again it was me who asked you to jump in headfirst in your first start-up.'

I caught myself smiling with my eyes closed.

'I have watched you struggle just to fit in. I've seen you victorious when you win over your own mind, and also watched you fall prey to your own mind in the moments when you cared too much about others' opinions.

'You say all this, but you weren't around many times,' I protested meekly. 'Where were you in some of my weak moments?'

'I have accompanied you in your most frivolous and most profound pursuits. The decibel of my voice almost fades with the background noise when you're stuck in the objects of senses—chasing some small pleasure here or running after fulfilling some insignificant desire there. However, the minute you snap out of that spiral, you hear me loud and clear.'

'Do you recall what Gurudev once said about three aspects of a spiritual path? Buddha, the awakened one. Dharma, your true nature, and Sangha, your tribe on the spiritual path. All three are essential in life. In your case, it was I who cajoled you into keeping your attention on the master and kept you from running away from the Sangha. It was only through our endless conversations that you even got some clarity about your Dharma.'

'Did I not push you out of your own concepts around having a guru? You know it and yes, you're welcome. Just know that I am always pointing you towards your North Star. Towards what is.'

'You have often let me guide you, although you followed my lead only at your convenience. Every time you didn't listen to me, you gave me another opportunity to swing by later and say, "I told you so!" But somewhere I feel you still don't get it fully. You keep going back to your conditioned mind. But it is completely fine. There is no conflict there. You do your thing and I do mine.'

'Getting you to move past your doubts was quite some challenge. I felt the pain of Sisyphus who was tasked to roll a huge stone uphill. I never give up though.'

'But I am proud of you,' he said. 'You remained persistent. You doubted the light, but you still kept going back to it. Until the point the veil of darkness vanished. Until your head made way for the heart. Until you cried tears of gratitude. Until you realized what really matters at the end of the day. It is a journey after all.'

'I may not always appear logical because I am not. I am beyond rationale. Doesn't it feel just right though when I speak to you?'

'I am Banka. I am your inner voice. I am you.'

Visible Invisible Hand

There is a silent voice that whispers to me in my weaker moments. It says, 'I'm with you. Wherever you are.'

As I walk on the promenade by the Hudson River on a breezy autumn evening, I cannot help but look back and reflect upon this wild ride. One that I would not trade for anything.

It is said that when one is ready, the master appears. But in my case, he showed up long before I was ready. Or should I say, long before I thought I was ready. He showed up and patiently waited until I was ready. Perhaps that is what showing up really looks like.

It is like a friend who has come to pick you up and drive you home. He waits patiently in the car outside while you are getting ready. You take hours to get ready, and he is still smiling warmly when you finally get to the car.

A friend like that perhaps exists only in one's imagination. I feel grateful for the infinite patience that Gurudev has shown for me to wake up to this reality. And I know he would continue to be there unconditionally if I needed more time.

Looking in the rear-view mirror, life seems like a mystery—dotted with wild coincidences, strange encounters and at times the most unpredictable outcomes. During the time that events were in the process of revealing themselves, it was difficult for me to see anything strange or uncharacteristic about them. Like the waves on the shore, events kept flowing in and out of my life. And each of these events created some outcome or effect—sometimes favourable and sometimes unfavourable. And that effect became the cause of the next event.

While there is always a cause for every effect, how does one pinpoint the specific cause for the noticed effect?

So then, is Gurudev's influence in my life the cause of some personal growth, or simply an effect of some preordained happening? Perhaps fate, probability, and everything in-between. Was there a force choreographing this entire experience?

In the year 1993, I was an engineering student back in India. Once, while crossing the Nehru bridge on my bike, I noticed the peeling light blue walls of the bridge masked by silver writing. Several small signs placed all over the bridge that read 'Jai Gurudev'. I imagine Gurudev must have been in my hometown around that time. I was immediately attracted to those words, although they meant little at that point. I hadn't even heard of Gurudev. I distinctly remember a warm and fuzzy feeling, but my mind was quick to discard the impulse to explore anything further. I didn't act upon it. I wasn't ready.

Clearly, before I met Gurudev, I had never imagined that someone like this would come in my life and flip the rudder. It started out with simple curiosity. Wanting to know him. To figure him out. To measure him up. And then somewhere along the way, I realized that there was no 'how' or 'why'. As I got closer and closer to the master, the plot thickened. On one hand, the mystery deepened, and on the other hand, the complexities of life began melting away. My chattering mind began taking more frequent breaks. Small things stopped mattering. My fears dropped away.

Around him, the mind stays in the moment. A complete state of *koviashuvik*—an Eskimo word for 'living in the present moment with quiet joy and happiness'. Despite all my quirks and shortcomings, I am accepted just as I am.

The funniest thing is that even after all this, I still have no idea who he really is and how all of this happened. I can only wonder.

'Sri Sri, who are you?' someone once asked at one of his talks at the All Souls Church in Washington DC.

At some level, life has simply been the journey to come to terms with my internal ground zero—my mind. Just like in the art of aerial warfare, instead of going after individual aircraft, you first focus on destroying the enemy's airstrip. The mind, however, is not an easy target.

I consider myself fortunate to have found a master who gave me tangible tools to navigate the maze of my own mind. Once out of this maze, you descend twelve inches. From the head to the heart. It has taken me over fifteen years, and I'm still enjoying the free fall.

I pause briefly and look up at the Manhattan sky. The gaping hole in the skyline has now been filled with an array of shiny glass and steel structures. And likewise, the hole in my soul has been filled with clarity and a sense of purpose. The pointed spire on the top of the freedom tower is trying to touch the sky.

Walking past the flowing river, it strikes me how everything in creation functions according to its nature, its Dharma. The nature of a river is to flow. Likewise, a human being's true nature is to love. And that which is our nature cannot change. But as Gurudev says, the expression of love changes. After all, a terrorist is also deeply in love with his misguided indoctrination. One gets angry because they are in love with perfection. All negative emotions are nothing but a distorted form of love. The loss and destruction that follow are real, and there can be no denial or justifications, but perhaps love is the only why and how.

Sometimes, it is all a matter of a subtle shift in perspective. Once, a student of the Zen tradition found himself on the bank of a flooded river. The bridge had been destroyed by the force of the water. The student called out to the master on the opposite bank, 'Master, how do I get to the other side?'

The master responded, 'You are already on the other side.'

'When you know who you are, you will know who I am,' Gurudev had replied to the curious gentleman in Washington DC that evening.

In the quest to know Gurudev, somewhere unknowingly I had started a quest to know myself. Will I find the answer in this lifetime? Or perhaps in as many lifetimes as there are leaves on all the trees along the promenade by the Hudson River? The logical mind has no answer. I don't need an answer. I have him.

We are all in the middle of a collective shift in consciousness. There is a *Tao*—the supreme order of the universe—lurking behind the apparent chaos and confusion in the world. I have no way to quantify. But I do feel the warmth of the light from a beacon that is quietly and patiently working towards affecting this fundamental change.

Some of the most powerful forces of nature are invisible and intangible. Gravity, friction, mind, love, self. Gurudev is that visible force, which helped me connect with the invisible Self. Like a gust of wind that makes one feel the presence of the otherwise invisible air.

Gurudev has dedicated his life to help and uplift humanity. And it all starts by giving people a glimpse of who they really are, by uniting them with what is. It only takes one experience to see life from an entirely different perspective. This is his mission. And perhaps mine is to contribute in whatever minuscule and insignificant way I can.

The Hudson is flowing gently, unaffected by the hustle on the island of Manhattan along the way.

Epilogue

I can't imagine anyone who hasn't experienced hair-raising turbulence at least once in their lifetime. Perhaps it's a gradual descent into chaos. Too often it's a nosedive. Such events leave deep scars on our nervous system, often manifesting as anger, depression, disbelief and fear. At some point, this turbulence often leads to a strange sense of void. A question arises from deep within. What is the point of all this?

Facing this emptiness is never easy. Especially when it's quiet around. It looks piercingly into your eyes. Its icy breath doesn't even quiver. There is something horrifying about this blackness. One misinformed way to get rid of it is by staying distracted. By avoiding it. By running the clock on this emptiness. I had tried it all and failed miserably.

Gurudev then taught me how to hack into the code of that void. By making amends with my reality instead of shunning it. By shaking hands with it. By fully embracing it and penetrating deep within it, instead of distracting myself away from it. An approach often unpleasant yet liberating.

But just when you think you've figured it all out, time throws you a curve ball.

Towards the end of ominous 2020, I abruptly lost my best friend, confidante and my unconditional support in every endeavour of life—my father. I watched helplessly as the universe swiftly took him away from us. Time spent with him felt like a dream that was now over.

Once again, the unsettling turbulence, and the much familiar void, returned. Only this time it was a lot more intense.

I once again felt like a lost World War II pilot, searching for a way home in a tattered plane, hoping and praying that somehow it would land. Rudders damaged beyond repair, the nose shattered and the engines heaving oil and flames. I was trying to land on a wing and a prayer.

My knee-jerk reaction, once again, was to find a way to get out of this pain quickly. The muscle memory of my mind wanted to pin me down into despair. But this time, I stayed the course with the void just like Gurudev had shown me. It was uncomfortable. Intense. Excruciating. Helplessness and longing created a spontaneous cry of help to the universe.

My practices provided much needed strength. Gurudev's wisdom felt like wind beneath my wings. The turbulence began to fizzle. The void now had a texture to it. There was an unmistakeable feeling of warmth within this void. Just like that in my father's embrace.

Jai Gurudev! Victory to the Big Mind!
May you never blink while flying into your own void.

Gratitude

Gurudev, for giving me this opportunity to be useful. For being the eternal light. My forever gratitude for everything there is.

Kristi Subramanian, you and your spreadsheets are a force of nature that kept me going. You played such a pivotal role in taking this book to the finish line. Thank you for patiently supporting all my crazy ideas, for your obsessive attention to details and for keeping things on track against a ticking clock. Deepest gratitude . . .

Vicky Block, you are such a writer at heart. Words can't express my thanks. I have learned so much from you—whether you'll agree with me or not.

James Nestor and Emma Seppälä for your invaluable guidance every single time I reached out. Thank you for being there!

Carol Kline, Michael Fischman, for the timely advice and for shining light on dark corners of this consuming process of bringing a book to life.

Rajshree Patel, for all the wisdom and love. For pushing me to look deep within and then some more.

Bill Herman, for encouraging me to trust the process and exchanging manuscripts. I can't wait.

Srividya Varchaswi, for all the love, support and counsel. Magic was inevitable from the day you stopped using my Amazon account and started helping me with the book.

Ashwin, Aditi and Rukun, they say you can't start the fire without a spark. You get it.

Jeff Houk, Bill Hayden, thank you for sharing your experiences and helping me connect dots in the history.

Ruchira Roy, Sandeep Karode, Swapnil Desai for your support on this writing journey.

Nikunj and Shruti, Archi, Aniket and Ruchika, for being the rocket boosters on the last lap. You guys!

Tarini Uppal, my editor, for infinite patience and handholding. So grateful for your support.

Kanishka Gupta, thank you for being you and trusting the newbie author in me.

Thank you everyone who gave me unfiltered feedback and your time throughout the process. I can only count my blessings. You know who you are!

And you Alak, for always being there. For never sugar coating your feedback, for being patient and holding me accountable. Helping me connect dots whenever I missed the forest for the trees. For bringing in the scaffolding when writers block got too heavy. For being the silent force in my life.

Next Steps

If you have reached here by reading through the entire book, you perhaps would agree with me that you'll always find a reason to not meditate. But don't give in. No, it is not something you do when you have spare time. When you meditate, you make time.

I would like to gift you three months of digital membership of the Art of Living Journey app. You can sign up on aolf.me/WingAndPrayerApp with the code WINGANDPRAYERAPP.

I also recommend that you learn SKY Breath Meditation, if you haven't already.

It is an effective and evidence-based powerful breath-meditation practice. An empowering technique that works like a natural instant stress reliever. Learned over three days, using specific rhythms of breath, it will quiet the mind and lead you into effortless meditation.

Research also shows that emotions are linked to breathing patterns and that you can change how you feel with your breath. The interesting part is that when you change the way you breathe, you can change your emotions. It's a two-way street. By changing your breath, you can change how you feel.

SKY Breath Meditation is shown to reduce stress and anxiety, improve sleep, boost the immune system, and restore energy. It has demonstrated results in more than 100 independent, peer-reviewed studies. And what's even better is that some results can be seen from the very first session.

I facilitate SKY Breath Meditation sessions on behalf of the Art of Living Foundation. It is my way of paying it forward by volunteering my time.

Come and learn this powerful breathwork technique with me.

Sign up for the program on www.kushalchoksi.com.

As a reader of this book, you can use 10 per cent discount code WINGANDPRAYER towards any SKY Breath Meditation program offered in the US.

You can also visit www.artofliving.org in your respective country and find a program that suits you.

Are you interested in scientific research on SKY? Please visit aolf.me/SKYResearch.

If you have any questions or feedback, please write to me at onawingandaprayerbook@gmail.com.

I look forward to hearing from you, sharing with you all I have learned and supporting you on your inward journey!